# Dynamic Oracle Performance Analytics

## Using Normalized Metrics to Improve Database Speed

Roger Cornejo

Apress®

*Dynamic Oracle Performance Analytics: Using Normalized Metrics to Improve Database Speed*

Roger Cornejo
Durham, NC, USA

ISBN-13 (pbk): 978-1-4842-4136-3          ISBN-13 (electronic): 978-1-4842-4137-0
https://doi.org/10.1007/978-1-4842-4137-0

Library of Congress Control Number: 2018965195

Managing Director, Apress Media LLC: Welmoed Spahr
Acquisitions Editor: Jonathan Gennick
Development Editor: Laura Berendson
Coordinating Editor: Jill Balzano

Cover image designed by Freepik (www.freepik.com)

Distributed to the book trade worldwide by Springer Science+Business Media New York, 233 Spring Street, 6th Floor, New York, NY 10013. Phone 1-800-SPRINGER, fax (201) 348-4505, e-mail orders-ny@springer-sbm.com, or visit www.springeronline.com. Apress Media, LLC is a California LLC and the sole member (owner) is Springer Science + Business Media Finance Inc (SSBM Finance Inc). SSBM Finance Inc is a Delaware corporation.

For information on translations, please e-mail rights@apress.com, or visit http://www.apress.com/rights-permissions.

Apress titles may be purchased in bulk for academic, corporate, or promotional use. eBook versions and licenses are also available for most titles. For more information, reference our Print and eBook Bulk Sales web page at http://www.apress.com/bulk-sales.

Any source code or other supplementary material referenced by the author in this book is available to readers on GitHub via the book's product page, located at www.apress.com/9781484241363. For more detailed information, please visit http://www.apress.com/source-code.

Printed on acid-free paper

*To Jeanne*

*About 35 years ago, you painted this quote
for me on a watercolor:*

*"Come grow old with me, the best is yet to be."
There are no regrets. It is a wonderful journey
with you by my side.*

# Table of Contents

# About the Author

**Roger Cornejo** has been an Oracle enthusiast since 1985 (versions 4–12c). He has many and varied experiences on large enterprise class Oracle applications, not only in performance troubleshooting and tuning but also in systems architecture, information modeling, and software development/project management. For the past ten years, Roger's main focus has been database performance analysis and tuning, with much of his time spent exploring the complexities and usefulness of AWR* tuning data. In his work, Roger is relied upon to produce Oracle database tuning results across 18c/12c/11g/10g (and occasionally 9i) databases. Roger is a thought-leader in his field and has been recognized for his expertise in tuning through such opportunities as presenting at the past eight East Coast Oracle Conferences, as well as at COLLABORATE14 and COLLABORATE18, RMOUG16, and Hotsos 2017–2018.

# About the Technical Reviewer

 **Bill Padfield** is an Oracle Certified Professional, working for a large telecommunications company in Denver, Colorado, as a senior database administrator. Bill helps administer and manage a large data warehouse environment consisting of more than 100 databases. Bill has been an Oracle database administrator for more than 16 years and has been in the IT industry since 1985. Bill also teaches graduate database courses at Regis University and currently resides in Aurora, Colorado, with his wife, Oyuna, and son, Evan.

# Acknowledgments

When I first started this work about a year and a half ago, I had no intention of writing a book on the subject—I simply wanted a better way to analyze the thousands of Oracle performance metrics available. I'd like to thank my wife, Jeanne Cornejo, for encouraging me to write the book and for the many hours she spent working with me. Dynamic Oracle Performance Analytics is a big and somewhat complex topic; Jeanne, a physical therapist by profession, worked tirelessly throughout the writing to help me break the material down so that even a nontechnical person can understand it. If you've ever seen the Johnny English movie where he breaks out into what appears to be a mini-seizure whenever he heard the word "Mozambique," it kind of got that way for her with "DOPA."

I'd also like to thank my oldest son, David Cornejo (PhD Operations Research), who provided me with inspiration and ideas as to how to get started with a lightweight version for implementing some rather complex big data analytical techniques (which are easily implemented in the Oracle SQL language).

Jonathan Gennick from Apress deserves credit for recognizing the potential value of this material to a wider audience and for reaching out to me and helping me get started with the proposal. A special thank you as well to the technical reviewer, Bill Padfield, who stuck with the review even though some key points needed more fleshing out.

# Introduction

In the practice of performance tuning, change is inevitable. New techniques are created; old ones are updated. The volume of metrics, especially those contained in Oracle's Automatic Workload Repository (AWR), is multiplying almost daily. Despite the autonomous database, monitoring tools, and other similar tools, the level of expertise required to analyze database performance problems has increased. To survive and thrive in this field, innovation is everything. Nothing remains the same for long. We either innovate and adapt to change or change happens to us.

The purpose of this book is not simply to help you adapt to change but to equip you with a method of analysis that will enable you to thrive and even lead in the application of creative big data science methods for Oracle performance analysis and tuning.

Before I begin to tell you about a process that I think you will find very potent, albeit very different from what you might be currently using, I want to tell you about my background in performance tuning. I'd like you to know that I've seen a lot of change and I've been where many of you are.

I began using Oracle as a software developer in 1985 (version 4.1.4). One important aspect of my work was to ensure high performance of enterprise class applications, so tuning was a necessary part of the job. At that time, there was little to no Oracle internal instrumentation exposed to the average user, so tuning involved a lot of guesswork. I relied on a careful study of the application architecture and used custom instrumentation for coarse-grained metrics.

When Oracle began to introduce internal metrics to the users, they did this through a series of views called "dynamic performance views" but commonly referred to as "v$ views" since they are prefixed with "v$." The v$ views include a host of metrics, many of which will be familiar to tuning experts, including v$session, v$sqlarea, v$sysstat, and v$OSstat.

Like many of my tuning peers, I quickly embraced these metrics as a primary source of metrics for finding problems in databases that needed tuning. The v$ views provide values for metrics for near real time. They are useful for solving problems that are happening at the present time, but since the metrics are not persisted over time, they are not very helpful when solving problems that happened in the past. This, of course, constrained the kinds of problems that I could solve quickly or the reproducibility of the problems that I was trying to solve.

With Oracle's introduction of the bStat/eStat utilities, I could see what happened during an interval of time, but I still had to be present when the problem was occurring (see sidebar note on bStat and eStat utilities).

Oracle made an improvement to the v$ views and the bStat/eStat utilities mechanisms by providing StatsPack, which captured many of those metrics over time and then persisted historic values for the metrics. With this added capability, I could look at past performance even when the problem was no longer apparent [occurring on the database]. I took a similar approach to querying StatsPack data as I used with the v$ view counterparts.

---

Note on the bStat/eStat utilities: This is a much-antiquated approach provided by Oracle prior to version 7 where you manually start and end a performance evaluation period—"bStat" is short for begin snapshot and is run prior to evaluating some SQL for performance; "eStat" is short for end snapshot and is run at the end of the performance evaluation period. Together these tools provide performance metrics for the manual snapshot period.

---

About eight years ago, I became aware of the plethora of metrics persisted in Oracle's Automatic Workload Repository. AWR metrics are an even more potent problem-solving tool. Some people refer to AWR as "StatsPack on steroids" primarily because of the additional metrics provided by ASH (active session history), which give a very detailed picture of what is going on with active sessions, and these metrics are persisted over a very granular time period. AWR also includes some other metrics such as dba_hist_sysmetric_summary, which help to paint a more detailed picture of what is going on in the database. During this metamorphosis of performance metrics, Oracle maintained continuity by providing the same information, but giving it a similar name in the new version of data presentation. Figure 1 gives an example of some performance metric sources represented in the v$ views, StatsPack views, and AWR views.

| V$ Views | StatsPack Views | AWR Views |
|---|---|---|
| V$SESSION | | DBA_HIST_ACTIVE_SESS_HISTORY |
| V$ACTIVE_SESSION_HISTORY | | DBA_HIST_ACTIVE_SESS_HISTORY |
| V$SESSION_EVENT | | DBA_HIST_ACTIVE_SESS_HISTORY |
| V$IOSTAT_FUNCTION | STATS$IOSTAT_FUNCTION | DBA_HIST_IOSTAT_FUNCTION |
| V$LATCH | STATS$LATCH | DBA_HIST_LATCH |
| V$LOG | | DBA_HIST_LOG |
| V$METRICNAME | | DBA_HIST_METRIC_NAME |
| V$OSSTAT | STATS$OSSTAT | DBA_HIST_OSSTAT |
| V$SQLSTATS | STATS$SQL_SUMMARY | DBA_HIST_SQLSTAT |
| V$SQLTEXT | STATS$SQLTEXT | DBA_HIST_SQLTEXT |
| V$SYSMETRIC_SUMMARY | | DBA_HIST_SYSMETRIC_SUMMARY |
| V$SYSSTAT | STATS$SYSSTAT | DBA_HIST_SYSSTAT |
| V$SYSTEM_EVENT | STATS$SYSTEM_EVENT | DBA_HIST_SYSTEM_EVENT |
| V$SYS_TIME_MODEL | STATS$SYS_TIME_MODEL | DBA_HIST_SYS_TIME_MODEL |

***Figure 1.*** *This table provides an excerpt comparison of some useful v$, StatsPack, and AWR views*

I began to use the enormous warehouse of AWR data somewhat differently than most developers/DBAs I knew. Instead of looking at AWR reports (or ASH or ADDM reports) as an initial analysis step in the tuning process, I began my analysis by querying specific individual DBA_HIST views for detailed information that I believed would lead me to discover performance problems more quickly. I chose the metrics I wanted to look at based on the type of metric and my past experience of how useful that information was for problem solving. I became quite adept at selecting where to look in the AWR for solving specific problems. I refer to this approach of selecting specific metrics as a "small model approach" because it uses only a subset of all the data available. I found this small model approach self-limiting and not always effective or efficient. It required a lot of knowledge of where to look for solving specific problems and a good amount of trial and error. I was able to gain proficiency over time, but it was a difficult and sometimes tedious learning process.

All of the tuning resources I have evaluated to date use some variation of this small model approach. Again, I use the term "small model" because they all rely on a subset of the available metrics—a predefined set of metrics is put forward as being highly predictive of finding performance problems. These methods and metrics are put forth by people who have a wealth of experience, and I grant that they are very useful in identifying problems in the areas for which the metrics were designed, but the downfall of the small model approach is that the decreased visibility into the tens of thousands of available metrics results in a less complete, less accurate understanding of the performance problem.

The method of analysis presented in this book represents an innovative, step change paradigm shift away from the traditional methods of analyzing Oracle database performance data. The method I present leverages big data and advanced analytical techniques (using plain SQL code) so that instead of relying on a few hand-picked/favorite metrics, the performance tuner is able to draw on "all" the available data without being overwhelmed by sheer volume and lack of a clear starting point. By formatting the data in a particular manner (discussed in Chapter 3), the tuning professional can apply big data methods to a tremendous number of metrics to draw impactful, focused performance improvement conclusions.

The Dynamic Oracle Performance Analytics (DOPA) process I created substantially increases the number of metrics that can be included in the analysis while simultaneously reducing the complexity of the analysis by identifying the metrics most relevant for solving a particular performance tuning problem. It is a predictive modeling technique. It enables the performance tuning to be efficient, targeted, and specific. The tuner will be able to quickly, accurately, and consistently identify a "root cause" with confidence.

# PART I

# Performance Tuning Basics

# CHAPTER 1

# Performance Tuning Basics

Before we begin Chapter 1, let me introduce you to Part I of this book.

As discussed in the Introduction, all of the current practices I'm aware of that are typically used for performance tuning can be grouped into a category that I call a small model approach. The small model approach includes a variety of methods that I also refer to as traditional methods because they represent the way tuning has been accomplished since Oracle began instrumenting and exposing performance metrics. The amount of data available to tuners has increased greatly, but the methods for examining the metrics remain essentially the same.

All of the traditional methods rely on a subset of metrics chosen from the overwhelming number of metrics persisted by Oracle and stored in the AWR (Automatic Workload Repository) or other repositories in the case of v$ views, StatsPack, custom tools, and other third-party tools. Oracle gathers these metrics automatically in the background (while applications are running) and persists them into a repository that is known as AWR. In its raw form, AWR is a massive repository of historic performance metrics and statistics. In an effort to make that data sensible to the user, Oracle exposes many of these metrics, though not all, in various reports (e.g., AWR report, active session history (ASH) report, AWR compare report, etc.). They have also developed tools that use the collected metrics

© Roger Cornejo 2018
R. Cornejo, *Dynamic Oracle Performance Analytics*,
https://doi.org/10.1007/978-1-4842-4137-0_1

and advanced algorithms to help direct tuning experts in their efforts to address performance issues (e.g., the various advisors available with the Tuning Pack license).

The purpose of all traditional approaches is to pinpoint areas of low performance which can then be targeted for tuning. The metrics chosen for analysis are selected based on their usefulness for solving performance problems, but for any given incident, the performance problem may or may not be manifested in the particular set of predefined metrics exposed by the tool. In my experience, performance issues are different every time (despite patterns of issues), and each class of problem tends to manifest in a different set of metrics; so if the tool misses the metric, the tuner is left to navigate her own path through a tsunami of metrics to find the problem. Expertise can be gained in knowing which metric to choose for examination, but it is often a hunt-and-seek process that can be particularly discouraging to someone new to the field.

Now, let us move on to Chapter 1.

In this chapter, I will discuss briefly a few of the most common traditional methods/tools used by performance tuners and how they can be useful. I'll mention their limitations as well in order to set the stage for the introduction of the DOPA process. This dynamic process is able to provide a more robust predictive analysis based on a much greater data source and to do so quickly and with proven impact. I've chosen the following four traditional approaches to discuss because they are the most frequently used by tuning experts.

# OEM

OEM is shorthand for Oracle Enterprise Manager Cloud Control 13c. When I refer to OEM, I usually mean the performance pages of OEM. OEM includes metrics contained in active session history (ASH) and other DBA_HIST views related to ASH (including DBA_HIST_SQLSTAT, DBA_HIST_SQL_PLAN) as well as metrics from a variety of other sources. I have found OEM most helpful for detecting problems in the top resource-consuming SQL statements that may require tuning. For example, the OEM ASH Analytics page will enable you very quickly to identify the SQL statements that are consuming the most resources. Generally, if you can tune this SQL, you can get better performance.

Figure 1-1 is an example of an ASH Analytics page from within OEM. It shows the top running SQL statement for the database in question to be sql_id 61afmmp6x53p5 [a sql_id is the primary identifier that Oracle uses to identify a SQL statement; refer to the Oracle documentation for more details]. This top running SQL statement is taking significantly more time than the next longest running SQL statement. Navigating around the ASH Analytics page in OEM, you can easily see the top SQL statements and find out what it/they are waiting on; in this case sql_id 61afmmp6x53p5, I was waiting on event, "db file sequential read," which is essentially indexed I/O.

By clicking on the hyperlink for the SQL ID in the ASH Analytics page (Figure 1-1), I can drill even deeper to the SQL Details page, and this SQL runs every five minutes and already has a custom SQL Profile on it. An example of the SQL Details page is in Figure 1-2. You can see in the figure that the statement being examined runs every five minutes and that there is a SQL Profile defined for it [in the section labeled "General," field labeled "SQL Profile"]. Note: SQL Profiles are sometimes provided by SQL Tuning Advisor as a solution to a SQL performance problem; it essentially fixes the execution plan through hints persisted outside the SQL statement. I refer the reader to the Oracle documentation on SQL Profiles for more details.

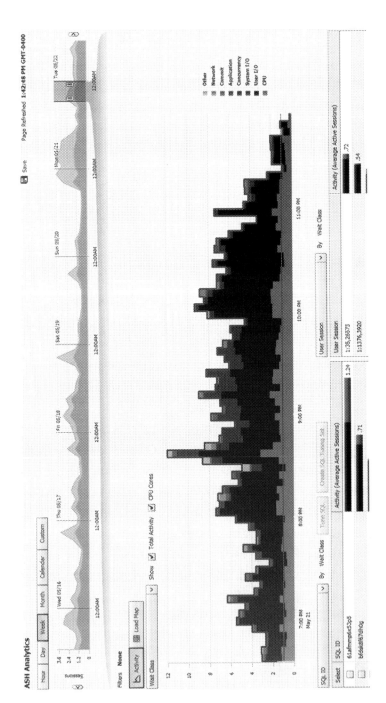

*Figure 1-1. Example ASH Analytics page from within OEM*

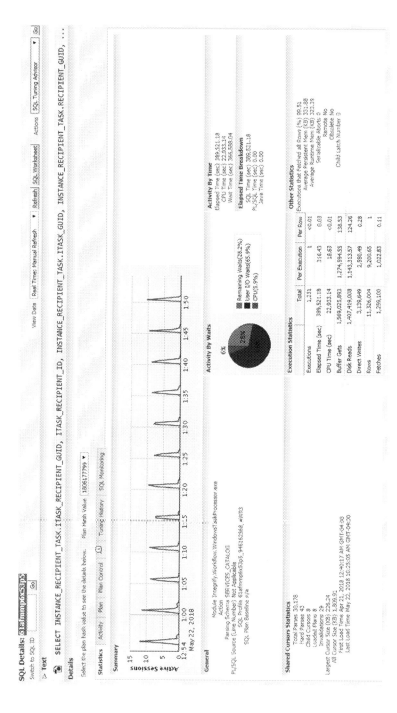

**Figure 1-2.** *Example SQL Details page*

OEM is very easy to use for top SQL analysis. Because OEM is easy to run and because SQL is fairly easy to tune (when the SQL Tuning Advisor provides actionable advice), many tuners jump right in and automatically tune the top SQL statement thinking that if a database is running a particular SQL statement a lot, then it must be at least a part of the performance problem. However, this is just not true in most of the performance cases I've worked on.

First of all, in my experience, application sessions running in the background (rather than sessions running application front-end SQL statements) are usually the source of top SQL, and this background work is almost never the source of the users' complaint. Their complaint is usually related to some business function in the online portion of the application that is not meeting the performance requirements. To the extent that tuning the top SQL statements will improve performance of these background processes and therefore reduce load on the machine, tuning top SQL can be helpful, but tuning top SQL when the chief problem lies elsewhere just won't fix the problem that the users are experiencing.

For example, in the preceding problem interval, users were complaining about a bit of SQL running from their reporting application that was taking approximately a minute and a half to execute, but the performance requirements were on the order of a few seconds. The users knew the time frame of the poor performance, the connect account name, and the module/machine name running the code. In this case, the SQL was not easy to identify using OEM because it wasn't a top resource-consuming SQL statement. When I used a custom query against DBA_HIST_ACTIVE_SESS_HISTORY, I was able to identify the sql_id. I ran that SQL statement through the SQL Tuning Advisor which recommended two new indexes [refer to the Oracle documentation for details on how to run the SQL Tuning Advisor]. Once these indexes were implemented, users saw a 90% performance improvement.

Another performance issue I encountered where the OEM/ASH Analytics use case did not identify the problem was when a user's session was stuck on an idle wait event (SQL*Net message from client). Again, using a custom SQL statement against the session history, I was able to identify the issue. As it turns out, this was a query across a database link and something happened to the remote session. For this problem, the solution was simple—kill the session and restart the query.

# ASH Reports

The ASH report embodies a problem-solving approach similar to OEM ASH Analytics page in that it targets SQL tuning by focusing on the top SQL statements for a session. Both of these tools can be useful when the source of the problem is a SQL statement. Both tools target SQL tuning by identifying the top resource-consuming SQL statements running on a database. The shortfall of ASH reports is similar to those already discussed for OEM. In both cases, if the problem is other than the top SQL, the problem will be missed using these tools.

I have observed that less battle-hardened/seasoned tuners often grab the top SQL and declare it/them to be the problem and then go about trying to fix it/them—but, as I discussed in the preceding section on OEM, just because a SQL statement ran often or long doesn't mean it was a cause of the poor performance being reported by the application users. When SQL tuning is the cause of poor performance, we want to identify not the longest running SQL but the SQL that is actually causing the performance problem. Spending time tuning a top SQL statement when that is not the real problem is a time waster; several fix/test cycles may pass before you are able to hone in on the real problem (if you ever get there).

While I was still using traditional approaches, I found both tools, OEM and ASH reports, cumbersome to use because, while they are good for the use cases for which they are designed (identifying top SQL), they were not helpful for most of the performance problems I encountered on a daily basis. Only a small percentage of the problems I see are caused by the top SQL. I improved upon these tools by developing custom code to directly query the AWR data for many of the same metrics contained in OEM and ASH reports with the slightly different purpose of finding the slowest SQL involved in a reported slow process, instead of the top SQL overall for the instance. My code allowed me to subset at a more granular level giving me greater flexibility, and this enabled me to focus in on the problem quickly. I have done several professional presentations on the method I used for tuning with this and other tools that I developed. I won't digress to discuss them in detail here since evaluation of SQL performance is incorporated into the more comprehensive DOPA process presented in this book and much more effectively accomplished by it.

OEM/ASH Analytics and the ASH report were designed to identify top SQL. When used for this purpose, they are effective tools. They are not, however, an effective or efficient starting point for tuning in general. This is because they only identify top SQL. There is a high potential for lack of alignment with the reported performance problem as the preceding examples demonstrate. An even greater concern is that many causes of performance degradation have nothing at all to do with SQL, and these will be missed entirely using these tools.

# AWR

The AWR is the Cadillac of data sets. It is also the tsunami of data sets. The AWR report exposes roughly 50 AWR data views containing tens of thousands of metrics, but to a great extent, the report lacks an interpretive component. Whereas the problem with OEM and ASH reports was that they were too narrowly focused and therefore useful for only a particular type of problem-solving use case, the data collected in the AWR is comprehensive and can tell you about every conceivable problem on the database, but the sheer volume of data is incredibly overwhelming. Consequently, you have to choose what metrics to look at. You also have to know what each metric measures and what kind of value it is indicating (time, percent usage, cumulative, etc.), and you have to know where to find it.

I have talked to many database analysts about AWR, and the most common remark I hear is that it is so overwhelming they don't know how to use it or where to start. I've met very few people who are proficient at using it. There are a few easily identifiable sections that most tuners adopt as their go-to sections, but most of the AWR is ignored.

If a tuner wanted to attempt to use AWR, he/she might start by trying to understand a particular metric. Some documentation exists, but much of AWR is not well documented. Even where documentation does exist, you might need to piece information together.

For example, the load profile section of AWR shows a line item "Redo size (bytes)" as pictured in Figure 1-3. There is a column for this variable in the AWR report showing Per Second and Per Transaction values. I discovered thru my own investigation that this is really a compilation of two metrics:

- Redo size/sec which is collected from Sys Metric Summary where its metric name is "Redo Generated Per Sec"

- Redo size/transaction which is collected from Sys Metric Summary where its metric name is "Redo Generated Per Txn"

**Load Profile**

| | Per Second | Per Transaction | Per Exec | Per Call |
|---|---|---|---|---|
| DB Time(s): | 0.0 | 0.3 | 0.01 | 0.02 |
| DB CPU(s): | 0.0 | 0.1 | 0.00 | 0.01 |
| Background CPU(s): | 0.0 | 0.1 | 0.00 | 0.00 |
| Redo size (bytes): | 3,032.5 | 25,926.3 | | |
| Logical read (blocks): | 353.3 | 3,020.5 | | |
| Block changes: | 16.8 | 143.5 | | |
| Physical read (blocks): | 67.8 | 579.4 | | |
| Physical write (blocks): | 6.5 | 55.8 | | |
| Read IO requests: | 4.6 | 39.1 | | |
| Write IO requests: | 0.5 | 4.6 | | |
| Read IO (MB): | 0.5 | 4.5 | | |
| Write IO (MB): | 0.1 | 0.4 | | |
| IM scan rows: | 0.0 | 0.0 | | |
| Session Logical Read IM: | | | | |
| User calls: | 1.7 | 14.9 | | |
| Parses (SQL): | 2.7 | 23.1 | | |
| Hard parses (SQL): | 0.1 | 0.4 | | |
| SQL Work Area (MB): | 0.3 | 2.4 | | |
| Logons: | 0.1 | 1.0 | | |
| Executes (SQL): | 3.7 | 31.6 | | |
| Rollbacks: | 0.0 | 0.0 | | |
| Transactions: | 0.1 | | | |

***Figure 1-3.*** *An example load profile section from an AWR report showing a line item "Redo size (bytes)"*

Knowing the variable name and where it comes from is a first step, but you also have to know what is being measured and how that information can be useful. The analyst must bring a knowledge of computer science and Oracle architecture in order to make sense of the metrics.

Another level of difficulty lies in the fact that raw numbers must be interpreted. Even if the analyst has a good knowledge of computer science and understands the metric, he has to determine if the value reported is indicative of a problem. Returning to Figure 1-3, an analyst would probably be able to guess that the Redo size metric is some measure of update activity against the database in bytes, but I don't think most would be able to tell you if this is a normal number or if it is indicative of a problem.

Most people who use the AWR data choose to learn about a few metrics and use them regularly. Perhaps they heard a speaker say how useful it was. They get comfortable with their chosen metrics and rely on them whenever analyzing a performance problem. This is what I did when I used a traditional approach for tuning; I had my go-to metrics for solving problems.

Using the metrics in AWR may be the best way to find any performance problem on any database, but using all of the metrics is humanly impossible. Which metrics to choose for solving a problem is the challenge. A select few favorites may enable you to get it right the first time, every time, but more often it is a process that requires very skillful navigation and multiple levels of investigation to be able to hone in on a problem. Even with an educated selection of metrics to begin with, there is usually some trial and error, narrowing down of the problem, eliminating some areas, and focusing on others. It's a process that requires many important decisions along the way. A skillful tuner can navigate quickly using the parts of AWR that are most useful for a given problem, but the novice will probably be quickly overwhelmed.

# ADDM

Unlike the AWR report, which has no interpretive component, the Automatic Database Diagnostic Monitor (ADDM) is designed to be an analytic tool. Oracle Corporation describes ADDM as "a revolutionary, first-of-its-kind performance self-diagnostic solution." ADDM interprets stats collected/reported by the AWR framework and analyzes them in regard to the top SQL statements and wait events [beginning in version 12c, Oracle includes the high-level findings from the ADDM report in the AWR report]. The goal of the ADDM analysis is to optimize database time; thus, long-running/high resource–consuming processes are identified as "problems." ADDM will often direct you to run further investigations on these "problems" (usually SQL Tuning Advisor or Segment Tuning Advisor). It will also frequently generate "solutions." The ADDM solutions most frequently involve parameter changes, specifically increasing SGA or PGA or log buffer.

When I was tuning using a traditional approach, I found the ADDM to be a valuable tool as have many other tuners. The metrics contained in it are extremely useful for identifying many problems that can affect performance, and the actionable advice is often profitable. However, once again, this tool has its limitations.

One problem with the ADDM that I frequently encounter is a scenario in which the problem SQL is not identified as one of the top SQL statements in the ADDM analysis. In these cases, the ADDM totally misses the problem SQL and will therefore not address the SQL statements that are key to solving the specific performance problem that has been reported. In this situation, an inexperienced tuner might take the SQL statements highlighted by the ADDM and spend time tuning SQL that have nothing to do with the real issue. The reason for this "deficiency" in the ADDM tool is its inability to evaluate a specific problem at a level detailed enough to give really useful information for that problem. That is, ADDM looks at the entire database, not a specific issue, and quite frequently, application performance issues are with SQL far below the top 5. I learned to view the ADDM as most useful for identifying "low-hanging fruit" because it is generally the case that if you tune SQL identified by the ADDM, you will get some performance improvement, but this improvement may or may not be significant. More importantly, as I've already mentioned, it may not even address the real problem, even if the real problem is SQL related.

Another shortcoming of the ADDM is that not all ADDM tuning advice will yield meaningful performance impact. If actioned unquestioningly, performing all the tuning recommended by ADDM would supply lots of busy work for the tuning professional and add cost unnecessarily. For example, ADDM might recommend increasing memory. Much effort could be spent upgrading memory with negligible impact to the overall performance. This would be a waste of effort as well as a monetary loss since adding memory has a significant cost.

# Summary

Oracle Corporation designed AWR and the suite of tools that accompany it as part of their effort to provide a manageability framework to undergird a self-managing database. Their goal was/is to make out-of-the-box database tuning as effortless as possible, but the tools they've created do not replace the performance tuner. Just as medical technology has produced extremely advanced tools for surgical procedures, the metrics stored in the AWR must still be used by a skilled operator to achieve the best outcome.

The traditional approaches discussed represent some of the most commonly used tools for performance tuning. Each of them relies on a subset of the data available in the AWR to help the tuner resolve performance problems, and therefore I consider them small model approaches. The limitation with all of these traditional, small model approaches is that although they can be useful for some instances, the tuner has to know which tool to use for each different type of problem. It is just not possible for a single individual to look at all of the available data collected by Oracle, so he/she must choose. The effectiveness of his analysis will depend on making the right choice. A tuner with lots of experience may be able to "intuitively" know which tool to go to in response to a particular complaint and may be able to diagnose problems with some consistency. But for the novice, making the wrong choice may cause him to come up empty-handed, or it may lead him into tuning efforts that are nonproductive. For the novice using the traditional approach, learning almost always involves lots of failures and frustrations.

The difficulty of acquiring skill in performance tuning using the traditional approaches is made significantly greater by the fact that tuning must be learned on a "broken" system. When databases are "broken," tensions can be high and the stress real. That is not an optimum time to experiment with tools that may or may not produce results. Many newbies give up and choose a new career trajectory.

With each new version of Oracle, more and more metrics have been added. These metrics may be very helpful for diagnosing problems, but they are additions to what I have previously referred to as the AWR tsunami. If a tuner were to try to take in all the metrics in the AWR at once, it would be like trying to drink from a fire hose or worse. The additional metrics complicate even further the question, "Which metric do I consider and in what order?" It is just not humanly possible to consider the thousands of metrics available and so people choose their favorite. If human effort were the only alternative, the suggestion of considering all/most of the metrics instead of just a few hand-picked ones would be outlandish, but with the use of big data techniques, this is exactly what the dynamic process enables tuners to do and with very little effort. The dynamic process ushers in a technique that, unlike the small model approaches currently used, employs vast amounts of the available data. It is for this reason that I call the dynamic approach a complete model approach.

Now let us move on to Part II and Chapter 2.

# PART II

# The Dynamic Oracle Performance Analytics (DOPA) Process

# CHAPTER 2

# Gathering Problem Information

Before I begin Chapter 2, let me introduce Part II of this book, which is made up of Chapters 2–7.

When I began tuning Oracle databases and applications back in the mid-1980s, I was using the methods that were state of the practice at that time and then moved to the traditional methods and tools mentioned in Chapter 1 as they became available. For metrics-based analysis, I looked at data in individual tables/views—first in the v$ views, later the StatsPack views when they were introduced, and finally, beginning with version 10g, I considered metrics persisted in the AWR views. I researched and worked hard to understand the content and meaning of the various metrics. I relied heavily on input from users about when a problem occurred and what the symptoms were to make choices about where to look. Over time and with practice, I was able to improve my ability to quickly hone in on a problem by choosing the right metrics to consider. I was always concerned, however, that there were so many metrics being ignored/left out of the analysis. Although I felt confident in my ability to perform a root-cause analysis for the problems I addressed, I was certain that a more complete analysis would yield a better, more holistic picture of the database and what was going on "under the covers."

© Roger Cornejo 2018
R. Cornejo, *Dynamic Oracle Performance Analytics*,
https://doi.org/10.1007/978-1-4842-4137-0_2

I knew what I really wanted/needed was a more scientific method of tuning that would use all the data/metrics and that would point me to the problem instead of having to predetermine where to look, but it took me time to discover a better method. Following is a short recollection of the epiphanies that led me to the development of the DOPA process as it is today. This approach accomplishes much of what I hoped to accomplish, although I am working continually to improve the underlying code.

Shortly after beginning to use AWR data, I discovered the DBA_HIST versions of the v$Sysmetric_Summary, v$SysStat, and v$Sys_Time_Model views [the Oracle documentation provides a good starting point for the reader who wants more information as to the content of these views and the meaning of the metrics they contain]. These views have hundreds of normalized metrics in them. I hand-picked several metrics (about two dozen) from these views since there were way too many to use all of them given my process at the time. The metrics I chose were those that aligned to things like CPU, IO, memory, network, workload, and REDO—classes of metrics I knew could be helpful for analyzing performance problems. I coded a program that captured the metrics I wanted to look at and pivoted them out into a multicolumn tabular format for each time interval in the analysis period under consideration. This enabled me to view only "relevant" metrics in such a way that abnormalities could be more easily identified.

I used this collection and presentation of metrics for diagnosing performance problems for many years. It provided results most of the time. Because my work involves support of over 300 production Oracle instances with more than 2500 applications, I had thousands of tuning opportunities and gained a tremendous amount of experience. I discovered that my ability to provide metrics-based root-cause analysis using these hand-picked metrics became quite good over time, but still, I knew that in overlooking so many other metrics, I might be missing essential observations. I knew my analysis was never as fully informed as it could be and that this lack of information might result in a poor problem hypothesis and/or a lower quality solution.

About two years ago, my son was completing his PhD work in Operations Research. I was privileged to be able to converse with him and his cohorts as they discussed the work they were doing in big data analytics. I began to wonder how I might be able to incorporate some of the techniques they used on big data to take advantage of all the data stored in the AWR for my analysis instead of only using the subset of data that my finite mind was able to analyze/comprehend. It is my experience that one can use big data analytical techniques such as embodied in the DOPA process against Oracle performance metrics, whether they be from a data warehouse application or an online transaction processing application that is running on the database.

One basic problem faced by performance tuners is a lack of knowledge about what is "normal" for a given metric; it's hard to know when something is "out of whack" if you don't know what values you should expect for the metric. So, I began my experimentation by calculating the normal range (using the rule of thumb: +/–2 standard deviations from the mean) of a given metric and "flagging" any metric value that was outside that normal range. I did this first for the hand-picked metrics I had been using, and I also included a few metrics I knew had absolute values I could easily identify. Examples of these known metric values included items such as the following:

- CPU utilization: For optimal response time, you want it to be below 65%.

- Single-block read latency: Above 20 milliseconds is high.

This experiment was successful; it demonstrated to me that establishing a normal range and then identifying metrics whose values fell outside the norm was an effective strategy for predicting where performance problems could be found. However, because the calculation

had to be coded separately for every metric, scalability presented a
major obstacle to its implementation. I could evaluate more metrics than
previously, but individually coding the calculation for all the available
metrics was not feasible given the many thousands of AWR metrics
available.

The next step in my experimentation was to organize the data into
a normalized data structure prior to performing calculations instead
of pivoting it out into a traditional short-wide structure with multiple
columns per time interval as I had been doing. The normalized data type
is a data structure referred to as key-value pair (KVP). In this format, each
row of data represents the metric and its value for a given time instance.
Figure 2-1 shows an example of what this looks like.

| BEGIN_TIME | METRIC_NAME | VALUE |
|---|---|---|
| 05/21/2018 08:00:00 | Redo Generated Per Sec | 1,071 |
| 05/21/2018 09:00:00 | Redo Generated Per Sec | 1,056 |
| 05/21/2018 10:00:00 | Redo Generated Per Sec | 1,000 |

***Figure 2-1.*** *This is an example of the normalized key-value pair*
*(KVP) data structure. Note that each row in the KVP structure*
*represents the metric and its value for a given time instance.*

I applied the statistical calculation for normal range to the KVP format
and flagged anything outside of normal range. Eureka!

It was a simple progression to union in other metrics that already
existed in a normalized format, such as sys time model. Then, it occurred
to me that any metric could be normalized by simply unpivoting the
multicolumn tabular (MCT) structure out into a KVP (tall, skinny format).
This was the beginning of the DOPA process.

I began using my new toy right away to solve performance problems.
As time permitted, I implemented additional metrics.

The entire process I've outlined thus far is accomplished using SQL. There is no fancy coding or special language required. Everyone who touches a database knows how to "talk SQL" to his database, and therefore this method is accessible to anyone who desires to learn it.

What I've relayed is the thought process and experimentation that led to the development of the DOPA process. At my son's suggestion, I explored the area of taxonomies. Application of taxonomies to the DOPA process increased the usefulness of this process even further, so I've added this component to the process. Chapter 6 discusses this topic in depth.

In its current form, I find the Dynamic Oracle Performance Analytics (DOPA) method to be extremely effective and powerful, but I see this process and its implementation as still in its nascent form. The DOPA process as currently implemented is powerful, but I think there is much more potential that can be achieved. The process I have outlined provides a useful tool as is and a framework on which further work can continue. I am persuaded that further efforts will not only enhance its usefulness for tuning but may lead to use cases far beyond tuning; that is to say, in a generic sense, the DOPA process is for anomaly detection, and this approach would work against any instrumented metrics to which you can talk SQL. For this reason, I consider the dynamic process a work in progress.

The DOPA process overcomes the major limitations of the small model approach which has been the sole tool of tuners to date.

- It uses a vast number of the available metrics, instead of a subset of metrics.

- It avoids user "bias" in the selection of metrics.

- Because of the large number of metrics, tuners can be more confident that all potentially problematic areas have a representation in the analysis.

- This larger set of evaluation/metrics enables a greater predictive accuracy.

Having discussed how the DOPA process evolved and why it is superior to the traditional/small model approach, I want to proceed to explain the actual process. The DOPA process described in this book vastly expands the metrics that can be considered in the tuning analysis without overwhelming the performance tuner with irrelevant data. It does this by consistently applying the following steps, each of which will be examined and explained in further detail in the following chapters:

1. Step 1: Gathering Problem Information (Chapter 2)

2. Step 2: Data Preparation (Chapter 3)

3. Step 3: Statistical Analysis (Chapter 4)

4. Step 4: Feature Selection (Chapter 5)

5. Step 5: Taxonomy (Chapter 6)

Chapter 7, on building the model and reporting, will bring these steps together.

Chapter 8 will go into quite a few case studies to show the DOPA process in action.

In short, the Dynamic Oracle Performance Analytics (DOPA) process computes statistical normal ranges for the instrumented metrics (11,000 metrics instrumented from AWR thus far) and uses those normal ranges to flag the unusual metric values from a problem interval (i.e., feature selection). When evaluating a problem interval, the DOPA process is used to report the flagged out of normal metrics, sorting those metrics with the most unusual values to the top. Essentially, the DOPA process I've developed uses a single SQL statement to refine the set of all metrics within the retention period down to the metrics which have unusual values (mostly high values) for a given problem interval. Thus, rather than an analyst pre-selecting the metrics they want to look at, the DOPA process dynamically determines which metrics are likely to be key influencers on the performance issue.

The metrics are instrumented/made available to the DOPA process by first normalizing them (i.e., unpivoting from a multicolumn table structure to a key-value pair structure and computing delta values for metric sources when the source values are persisted as cumulative [covered in Chapter 3—Data Preparation]) and then unioning all the normalized metrics into a single "view." This "view" on instrumented metrics and their values is fed into the portions of the code that remove outliers (if present), calculates the normal ranges for each metric, and then does the flagging as described in the preceding text. The DOPA process also factors in the concept of a taxonomy (I built two taxonomies, an infrastructure taxonomy and an Oracle taxonomy) where metrics are assigned to higher level categories and subcategories within the taxonomy [the taxonomies help as they bundle the metrics into higher level categories for easier interpretation]. The flagged metrics can be reported in a variety of ways, but I use three views:

- Category Count View that counts flagged metrics by taxonomical category (this is helpful to provide a high-level view of the performance issue)

- Metrics Aggregate View which shows each flagged metric and their average values along with the normal ranges and other information that can be useful

- Metrics Time-Series View which I usually use to provide the time-series trend for a single metric

Since the DOPA process is looking at a very large number of dynamically flagged metrics, this can prevent the analyst from missing essential observations that would not be shown if metrics were pre-selected. Using the DOPA process, the analyst can develop a better hypothesis of the problem. Further, in many cases the set of expected values for a metric is not known by the DBA; the DOPA process provides metric value assessment in the process of computing the normal ranges.

Additionally, I have personally benefitted from using the DOPA process expanding my knowledge of tuning by doing additional research on a flagged metric that I have not yet seen. It is the task of the DOPA process user to exercise good judgment and decide what metrics or problem areas to focus on for further analysis.

Now, let's dig into Chapter 2.

To the database tuner, gathering information is a necessary first step in the process of identifying the root cause of a performance problem; actually, you can think of information gathering as a precondition. Database application users or support staff would like to simply tell us that "your" database isn't working and expect that we will know how to find and fix the problem. Trying to address a performance incident in an information vacuum is just not reasonable; obtaining some basic information about the performance degradation users are experiencing is essential to discovering the root cause and devising a tuning plan. An accurate diagnosis depends to a large degree on an accurate description of the problem. At the very least, accurate information will speed the tuning process; user description of the problem is a piece of the puzzle, and without it, the tuner is greatly handicapped. Accurate information is also vital because you want to make certain that you are addressing the performance degradation the user is experiencing and not another problem that might present itself, but for which no degradation has been reported. For example, tuning the top SQL [as previously described] can easily miss the problem being experienced by the users; this issue might be worthy of your attention, but the user complaint should always be the priority.

Because users are not familiar with the workings of the database but interact with it through applications that run on the database, the information they provide when reporting a performance incident can be quite faulty. Often users will express the nature of the problem they are experiencing in the language of the tool they are using to access the database. For example, they might give an Informatics job name or an application log with no interpretation. As database analysts, we often don't have experience interpreting application-specific messages/logs. We usually don't have a mapping from Informatics job name to something that occurs on the database. To overcome this difficulty, we need to ask users to translate the job name to the SQL that's running or at least provide a start/end time and an expectation of how long they think it should take because then we can look to see what was running during that time interval.

Sometimes users will have a performance problem but delay requesting help. If the delay is long, the problem interval may no longer be stored in the history data. In this case, it is necessary to wait until the problem reoccurs. In this situation, it's important to educate the user about the importance of a timely request so that future problems can be addressed quickly.

Another problem I have encountered is that users will try to "self-diagnose" a problem and/or use incorrect terms. For example, I had a user report that the database was "deadlocked." This term has a very specific meaning to a database professional, but when I questioned the user, it was clear that he was using the term to mean something very different (e.g., in this case, what he meant was "slow-running SQL"). This serves to show that you can't always take the user's description at face value or you may be running down rabbit holes.

These are just a few examples of the kinds of obstacles I have encountered in attempting to gain information from users about a particular problem. In order to overcome them and to standardize the information with which I begin my analysis, I have come up with a few basic questions for which I ask users to supply an answer if possible. I've listed those questions in the following text with a brief explanation about how this information may be relevant for the tuning process.

# Has This Run Before?

It's good to know if the poor-performing process is new. I see many cases where scalability testing was not done prior to production, and then when the application hits production scale for the first time, it falls over.

# When Did the Problem Start?

This will tell me the time interval that I need to look at for my tuning analysis. Since I work on databases that run applications for users across the globe, I always ask for the database timestamp which includes the time zone.

# What Was the Start and End Time of the Application Run?

When the time interval can be clearly identified (e.g., the problem occurred between 2p.m. and 3p.m. EST), it will necessitate a smaller analysis interval and hence a smaller data set than if a less-well-defined period is reported (e.g., the problem occurred yesterday). A more narrow interval will make it quicker and easier to find the problem.

# What Database Were You Connected To?

It's important to know the database name because in organizations that have many Oracle instances running, applications can be run on any of a number of different databases, and I need to be sure I am looking at the correct one.

# What User Accounts Are They Using to Connect to the Database?

There can be many users accessing the database for different purposes, and not all will necessarily be experiencing problems. On a large database, there could be hundreds of connect accounts. If I target just those metrics related to the connect account for the user reporting a problem, it will greatly reduce the data set for analysis.

# What SQL Do You Believe You Were Running?

Most of the time, users don't know the answer to this question. But they might be able to provide some hints that are useful. For example, they might say something like, "We were updating the Study table." That statement gives me two pieces of information that I can use. It tells me that the problem probably involves an update statement and that I'll want to be looking for a SQL statement that touched the Study table.

# What Is the Expected Duration?

I use the user's report of expected duration as the performance requirement. This will be my target for the tuning efforts. Performance requirement is sometimes, but not usually, included in the documentation of an application. To overcome this oft-missing information, I ask the user for the expected duration based on his/her previous experience with the system, as a proxy. This is information they are always able to provide.

# Did You Receive Any Oracle Error Messages?

Knowing if there is an Oracle error message and what those messages were is very important. An Oracle message can sometimes indicate that the problem is clearly not a performance issue. For example, a "duplicate value in index" message is not a performance problem; it indicates that the problem is with the application. In these problem types, the program abnormally ends with Oracle error message. Some Oracle error messages, however, do fall into the category of performance problems. For many error messages, ascertaining whether the error code is a result of performance issues will require further discovery. An example of this would be "TEMP tablespace" errors. A "TEMP tablespace error" could indicate a deficient amount of tablespace for the application which would be a configuration problem, but it might also indicate a problem with the execution plan which is causing too much tablespace to be used.

The questions I've noted thus far are part of a basic intake form that I ask clients to complete. In addition to this basic information, the following information may also be helpful if it can be obtained:

> sql_id / top level sql_id
>
> SQL text or part of the SQL text
>
> Machine/module/program/action
>
> Session_id, session_serial#,

What made you conclude that it is a database problem?

For some situations, it's helpful to have run details for when the application was behaving normally.

# Summary

To summarize, the purpose of the information gathering process is threefold:

- We want to be able to focus in on the performance degradation being experienced by the users.

- We want to confirm that we are looking for the problem in the right database.

- We want to be able to drive down to the session level as quickly as possible—this allows for the most efficient analysis because unless the analysis indicates there is a systemic problem, most of the tuning will be done at the SQL tuning level.

Before I began using the DOPA process, I would not even start to diagnose a problem until the users provided the information requested, or at least as much of it as they could. Since I have been using this tool, however, I have discovered that I can run the code and gain a very good idea of what the problem is with only the most basic information (database name and the approximate time interval). The DOPA process is so powerful and so capable that it can evaluate the available metrics and provide an operational profile of what is going on in the database, revealing what is unusual. The DOPA process puts so many of the pieces of the puzzle together that I am able to obtain a good notion of what the whole picture looks like even with only a scant problem description. Once the users provide the requested information, it's just a matter of filling in the gaps and completing the analysis.

The ability of the DOPA process to work even when given a poor description of the problem does not make the data collection process obsolete. Rather, it allows me to take a first analysis step. Additional information from the client will help me focus in on the problem area.

I want to illustrate this with an example:

I had a user complain of a hung process. While I was waiting for them to provide the requested information, I ran my DOPA process using an approximated interval. I could see from the results that there was a high level of idle waits on the network, so I had a good notion of where the problem was occurring. When I received the information from the user and a more detailed description, I quickly discovered they had a SQL statement that was sitting there doing nothing, just waiting for the network [a large-scale network outage impacted many SQL statements that were using database links (database links can be used in a SQL statement to query data from a remote database, or several remote databases, in a single query)]. We killed the process and restarted it and performance returned to normal.

Let us now move on to data preparation.

# CHAPTER 3

# Data Preparation

Information from the client related to the performance issue being experienced is an important element in determining root cause. This information can be viewed as a source of data for the analytic process. The other source of data that is invaluable to the analytic process is data obtained from the database itself. This chapter provides step-by-step instructions for how to collect and prepare the data from the database in preparation for the next step in the analysis process which is statistical analysis. The process of preparing data occurs in the following sequence:

- Identify the metrics you want to instrument (i.e., those metrics you choose to use that will provide the source data for the analysis)

- Normalize the metric data

- Convert cumulative data to deltas

- Union normalized metrics from multiple sources

**Identifying the metrics** you want to instrument is an obvious first step, but the choice of what data to use is almost limitless and therefore of no small consequence. In version 12c of Oracle, there are about 140 DBA_HIST views. When I began experimenting with this new process, I chose a handful of tables I wanted to incorporate. I chose tables from the AWR framework based on my experience/familiarity with them. I chose metrics/tables I had found helpful/indicative of performance issues in the

© Roger Cornejo 2018
R. Cornejo, *Dynamic Oracle Performance Analytics*,
https://doi.org/10.1007/978-1-4842-4137-0_3

past while I was using a traditional approach. As I expanded this effort, I continued to add tables/metrics. So far I have instrumented seven tables which include approximately 11,000 metrics. The collection of these metrics occupies approximately two million rows when the data collection is done in hourly increments over a week.

Figure 3-1 shows a list of the data sources I have instrumented thus far.

| Metric Source | Metric Count |
|---|---|
| dba_hist_iostat_function | 150 |
| dba_hist_sysstat | 1,178 |
| dba_hist_latch | 8,470 |
| dba_hist_osstat | 18 |
| dba_hist_system_event | 894 |
| dba_hist_sys_time_model | 29 |
| dba_hist_sysmetric_summary | 161 |
| Total | 10,739 |

***Figure 3-1.*** *AWR data sources and their metric counts as instrumented in the DOPA process as of this writing*

The dynamic approach does not limit you to these metric sources. You can add any metrics you wish, or remove some, by modifying the SQL statement you use to fetch them. For example, the metrics I plan to instrument next are:

dba_hist_waitstat: cumulative stats on block contention, including CLASS, WAIT_COUNT, TIME

dba_hist_undostat

custom queries: e.g., DBA_ADVISOR% ; DBA_HIST_SQLSTAT ;... blocked sessions

My DOPA process includes in the analysis Exadata and in-memory metrics since they are included in one of the metric source tables (DBA_HIST_SYSSTAT) from which I am pulling data. When Oracle introduces new features such as Exadata [Exadata is Oracle's database machine platform which has been available for many years] and database in-memory (introduced in Oracle 12c), they are also introducing a ton of new and useful metrics. Suffice it to say that the DOPA process is flexible enough to automatically incorporate many of these new metrics right off the bat.

The following figures show some of the metrics collected to support these features.

Figure 3-2 lists some of the in-memory metrics instrumented by the Oracle developers (198 total in 12c as of this writing).

| METRIC_SOURCE | METRIC_NAME |
|---|---|
| dba_hist_sysstat | IM repopulate segments requested |
| dba_hist_sysstat | IM repopulate transactions active |
| dba_hist_sysstat | IM repopulate transactions check |
| dba_hist_sysstat | IM repopulate undo records applied |
| dba_hist_sysstat | IM repopulate undo segheader rollback |
| dba_hist_sysstat | IM scan blocks cache |
| dba_hist_sysstat | IM scan bytes in-memory |
| dba_hist_sysstat | IM scan bytes uncompressed |
| dba_hist_sysstat | IM scan CUs cleanout |
| dba_hist_sysstat | IM scan CUs column not in memory |
| dba_hist_sysstat | IM scan CUs columns accessed |
| dba_hist_sysstat | IM scan CUs columns decompressed |
| dba_hist_sysstat | IM scan CUs columns theoretical max |
| dba_hist_sysstat | IM scan CUs failed to reget pin |
| dba_hist_sysstat | IM scan CUs invalid |
| dba_hist_sysstat | IM scan CUs invalid (all rows are invalid) |
| dba_hist_sysstat | IM scan CUs invalid or missing revert to on disk extent |
| dba_hist_sysstat | IM scan CUs memcompress for capacity high |
| dba_hist_sysstat | IM scan CUs memcompress for capacity low |
| dba_hist_sysstat | IM scan CUs memcompress for dml |
| dba_hist_sysstat | IM scan CUs memcompress for query high |
| dba_hist_sysstat | IM scan CUs memcompress for query low |
| dba_hist_sysstat | IM scan CUs no cleanout |
| dba_hist_sysstat | IM scan CUs no memcompress |
| dba_hist_sysstat | IM scan CUs no rollback |
| dba_hist_sysstat | IM scan CUs optimized read |
| dba_hist_sysstat | IM scan CUs predicates applied |
| dba_hist_sysstat | IM scan CUs predicates optimized |
| dba_hist_sysstat | IM scan CUs predicates received |
| dba_hist_sysstat | IM scan CUs pruned |

***Figure 3-2.*** *Sample of some key in-memory metrics persisted in DBA_HIST_SYSSTAT. The blog: blogs.oracle.com/in-memory explains in detail the key in-memory metrics*

Figure 3-3 shows a few of the approximately 69 metrics instrumented for Exadata.

| METRIC_SOURCE | METRIC_NAME |
| --- | --- |
| dba_hist_sysmetric_summary | Cell Physical IO Interconnect Bytes |
| dba_hist_sysstat | cell smart IO session cache lookups |
| dba_hist_sysstat | cell smart IO session cache hwm |
| dba_hist_sysstat | cell smart IO session cache hits |
| dba_hist_sysstat | cell smart IO session cache hard misses |
| dba_hist_sysstat | cell simulated physical IO bytes returned by predicate offload |
| dba_hist_sysstat | cell simulated physical IO bytes eligible for predicate offload |
| dba_hist_sysstat | cell scans |
| dba_hist_sysstat | cell physical write IO host network bytes written during offloa |
| dba_hist_sysstat | cell physical write IO bytes eligible for offload |
| dba_hist_sysstat | cell physical write bytes saved by smart file initialization |
| dba_hist_sysstat | cell physical IO interconnect bytes returned by smart scan |
| dba_hist_sysstat | cell physical IO interconnect bytes |
| dba_hist_sysstat | cell physical IO bytes sent directly to DB node to balance CPU |
| dba_hist_sysstat | cell physical IO bytes saved during optimized RMAN file restore |
| dba_hist_sysstat | cell physical IO bytes saved during optimized file creation |
| dba_hist_sysstat | cell physical IO bytes saved by storage index |
| dba_hist_sysstat | cell physical IO bytes saved by columnar cache |
| dba_hist_sysstat | cell physical IO bytes eligible for predicate offload |
| dba_hist_sysstat | cell partial writes in flash cache |
| dba_hist_sysstat | cell overwrites in flash cache |
| dba_hist_sysstat | cell num smartio transient cell failures |
| dba_hist_sysstat | cell num smartio permanent cell failures |
| dba_hist_sysstat | cell num smartio automem buffer allocation failures |
| dba_hist_sysstat | cell num smartio automem buffer allocation attempts |
| dba_hist_sysstat | cell num smart IO sessions using passthru mode due to user |
| dba_hist_sysstat | cell num smart IO sessions using passthru mode due to timezone |
| dba_hist_sysstat | cell num smart IO sessions using passthru mode due to cellsrv |
| dba_hist_sysstat | cell num smart IO sessions in rdbms block IO due to user |
| dba_hist_sysstat | cell num smart IO sessions in rdbms block IO due to open fail |
| dba_hist_sysstat | cell num smart IO sessions in rdbms block IO due to no cell mem |

***Figure 3-3.*** *This listing shows some of the key Exadata metrics persisted in DBA_HIST_SYSSTAT and DBA_HIST_SYSMETRIC_SUMMARY*

Since the databases on which I work typically don't have the Exadata or database in-memory licensed features, the returned value for these metrics is zero. However, if you are working on an Exadata machine or a database with the in-memory feature turned on and run the same code, there will be a result returned, and it will be incorporated into the analysis. By writing your code to always include these important metrics, you don't have to worry about missing relevant observations, and you don't have to rewrite code when machine licensing changes. When those metrics are available, they will be included in the analysis. When they aren't available, the returned value will be zero and they will not inform the analysis.

# Normalize the Data

As I related in the introduction to this section, while I was tuning using traditional methods, I found it useful to collect and pivot data out of the tables where they were found into a short, wide format for my performance tuning work. When I began trying to develop a new process for analysis, I found this short-wide data structure cumbersome to work with. I had to write separate code for each metric I wanted to include because each kind of measurement was a special case. This made scaling to thousands of metrics impossible. I realized that if I used the normalized data structure (key-value pair format—also described as a tall, skinny format) instead, I would have a common format for the data, and this would allow me to complete the analysis on all the metrics with just one SQL statement.

Normalization, therefore, is the second step in the process of data preparation. Normalizing the data structure involves putting the metric data into a format commonly referred to as key-value pairs. The normalized data structure looks like a tall, skinny table as opposed to the multicolumn table (MCT) that looks short and wide. Some of the AWR tables (e.g., dba_hist_sysmetric_summary and dba_hist_sys_time_model) already report the metrics they contain in a normalized view. The challenge then was to discover a way to convert the multitude of metric sources that are in a multicolumn table (MCT) structure to a normalized structure.

The process I use to normalize data involves logically "unpivoting" traditional short-wide structured data (MCT) into a tall, skinny structure of key-value pairs. In this format, each row is a key-value pair (KVP).

Figures 3-4, 3-5, and 3-6 show examples of data in both MCT and KVP formats. On the top of the figure, the data is displayed in a short-wide MCT format, and below that, the same data is displayed in a tall, skinny format (KVP).

Figure 3-4a shows the multicolumn table format of DBA_HIST_LATCH. A SQL "describe" can be used to see all the columns of DBA_HIST_LATCH.

The source SQL to produce Figure 3-4a follows.

```
with latch as
(
select * from dba_hist_latch
)
select SNAP_ID "SNAP ID", level# "LEVEL #", LATCH_NAME, GETS,
MISSES, SLEEPS, spin_gets "SPIN GETS", wait_time "WAIT TIME"
from latch
where latch_name like 'cache buffers chains%'
order by latch_name, 1
;
```

| SNAP ID | LEVEL # | LATCH_NAME | GETS | MISSES | SLEEPS | SPIN GETS | WAIT TIME |
|---|---|---|---|---|---|---|---|
| 48,124 | 1 | cache buffers chains | 1,322,612,364,217 | 125,330,608 | 936,130 | 124,449,858 | 429,013,207 |
| 48,125 | 1 | cache buffers chains | 1,323,911,548,190 | 125,349,459 | 937,648 | 124,467,236 | 429,418,612 |
| 48,126 | 1 | cache buffers chains | 1,326,158,175,028 | 125,387,243 | 942,316 | 124,500,418 | 431,257,121 |
| 48,127 | 1 | cache buffers chains | 1,327,522,956,363 | 125,401,078 | 942,589 | 124,514,006 | 431,463,017 |
| 48,128 | 1 | cache buffers chains | 1,328,777,096,698 | 125,414,174 | 942,912 | 124,526,794 | 431,742,790 |
| 48,129 | 1 | cache buffers chains | 1,329,872,261,126 | 125,434,774 | 944,729 | 124,545,607 | 432,280,506 |
| 48,130 | 1 | cache buffers chains | 1,331,338,278,421 | 125,441,531 | 945,052 | 124,552,075 | 432,544,136 |

***Figure 3-4a.*** *Multicolumn table format of DBA_HIST_LATCH*

Figure 3-4b shows DBA_HIST_LATCH "normalized" to the key-value pair format. This is accomplished by concatenating the latch name with each of the column names to form the metric name. The SQL source code to produce this figure follows.

```
with latch as
(
select * from dba_hist_latch
)
, unpivot_latch as
(
    select a.snap_id, a.latch_hash metric_id, LEVEL# || ': '
|| latch_name || ' gets' metric_name, gets cumulative_value ,
a.dbid, a.instance_number from latch a
union select a.snap_id, a.latch_hash metric_id, LEVEL# || ':
' || latch_name || ' misses' metric_name,  misses cumulative_
value , a.dbid, a.instance_number from latch a
union select a.snap_id, a.latch_hash metric_id, LEVEL# || ':
' || latch_name || ' sleeps' metric_name,  sleeps cumulative_
value , a.dbid, a.instance_number from latch a
union select a.snap_id, a.latch_hash metric_id, LEVEL# || ': '
|| latch_name || ' immediate_gets' metric_name, immediate_gets
cumulative_value , a.dbid, a.instance_number from latch a
union select a.snap_id, a.latch_hash metric_id, LEVEL# || ': '
|| latch_name || ' immediate_misses' metric_name,  immediate_
misses cumulative_value , a.dbid, a.instance_number from latch
a
union select a.snap_id, a.latch_hash metric_id, LEVEL# ||
': ' || latch_name || ' spin_gets' metric_name, spin_gets
cumulative_value , a.dbid, a.instance_number from latch a
```

```
union select a.snap_id, a.latch_hash metric_id, LEVEL# || ':
' || latch_name || ' sleep1' metric_name,  sleep1 cumulative_
value , a.dbid, a.instance_number from latch a
union select a.snap_id, a.latch_hash metric_id, LEVEL# || ':
' || latch_name || ' sleep2' metric_name,  sleep2 cumulative_
value , a.dbid, a.instance_number from latch a
union select a.snap_id, a.latch_hash metric_id, LEVEL# || ':
' || latch_name || ' sleep3' metric_name,  sleep3 cumulative_
value , a.dbid, a.instance_number from latch a
union select a.snap_id, a.latch_hash metric_id, LEVEL# || ':
' || latch_name || ' sleep4' metric_name,  sleep4 cumulative_
value , a.dbid, a.instance_number from latch a
union select a.snap_id, a.latch_hash metric_id, LEVEL# ||
': ' || latch_name || ' wait_time' metric_name,  wait_time
cumulative_value , a.dbid, a.instance_number from latch a
)
select snap_id, metric_name, cumulative_Value
from unpivot_latch
where metric_name like '%cache buffer%' order by 1,2
;
```

| SNAP_ID | METRIC_NAME | CUMULATIVE_VALUE |
|---|---|---|
| 48,124 | 1: cache buffers chains **gets** | 1,322,612,364,217 |
| 48,124 | 1: cache buffers chains **immediate_gets** | 5,241,518,517 |
| 48,124 | 1: cache buffers chains **immediate_misses** | 395,520 |
| 48,124 | 1: cache buffers chains **misses** | 125,330,608 |
| 48,124 | 1: cache buffers chains **sleep1** | 0 |
| 48,124 | 1: cache buffers chains **sleep2** | 0 |
| 48,124 | 1: cache buffers chains **sleep3** | 0 |
| 48,124 | 1: cache buffers chains **sleep4** | 0 |
| 48,124 | 1: cache buffers chains **sleeps** | 936,130 |
| 48,124 | 1: cache buffers chains **spin_gets** | 124,449,858 |
| 48,124 | 1: cache buffers chains **wait_time** | 429,013,207 |

***Figure 3-4b.***  *DBA_HIST_LATCH "normalized" to the key-value pair format*

Figure 3-5a shows the multicolumn table format of DBA_HIST_ SYSTEM_EVENT. A SQL "describe" can be used to see all the columns of DBA_HIST_SYSTEM_EVENT. You may note that here again the values in the various columns are cumulative rather being the value for just that particular snap_id.

The source SQL to produce Figure 3-5a follows.

```
with system_event as
(
select * from dba_hist_system_event
)
select snap_id, wait_class, event_name, total_waits, total_
timeouts , time_waited_micro
from system_event
where event_name like 'cursor: pin S wait on X'
order by 1,2,3
;
```

| SNAP_ID | WAIT_CLASS | EVENT_NAME | TOTAL WAITS | TOTAL TIME OUTS | TIME WAITED MICRO |
|---|---|---|---|---|---|
| 48,124 | Concurrency | cursor: pin S wait on X | 4,815 | 0 | 1,227,334,179 |
| 48,125 | Concurrency | cursor: pin S wait on X | 4,815 | 0 | 1,227,334,179 |
| 48,126 | Concurrency | cursor: pin S wait on X | 4,821 | 0 | 1,227,873,750 |
| 48,127 | Concurrency | cursor: pin S wait on X | 4,823 | 0 | 1,230,895,951 |
| 48,128 | Concurrency | cursor: pin S wait on X | 4,824 | 0 | 1,230,908,179 |
| 48,129 | Concurrency | cursor: pin S wait on X | 4,829 | 0 | 1,232,764,868 |
| 48,130 | Concurrency | cursor: pin S wait on X | 4,831 | 0 | 1,232,779,529 |

*Figure 3-5a.* Multicolumn table format of DBA_HIST_SYSTEM_EVENT

Figure 3-5b shows DBA_HIST_SYSTEM_EVENT "normalized" to the key-value pair format. This is accomplished by concatenating the wait class with the event name with each of the column names to form the metric name. The SQL source code to produce this figure follows.

```
with system_event as
(
select * from dba_hist_system_event
)
, unpivot_system_event as
(
        select a.snap_id, a.event_id metric_id, wait_class ||
': ' || event_name || ' total_waits' metric_name, total_waits
cumulative_value , a.dbid, a.instance_number from system_event a
union select a.snap_id, a.event_id metric_id, wait_class ||
': ' || event_name || ' total_timeouts' metric_name,  total_
timeouts cumulative_value , a.dbid, a.instance_number from
system_event a
union select a.snap_id, a.event_id metric_id, wait_class || ':
' || event_name || ' time_waited_micro' metric_name,  time_
waited_micro cumulative_value , a.dbid, a.instance_number from
system_event a
)
select snap_id, metric_name, cumulative_value
from unpivot_system_event
where metric_name like '%cursor: pin S wait on X%'
order by 1,2
;
```

| SNAP_ID | METRIC_NAME | CUMULATIVE_VALUE |
|---|---|---|
| 48,148 | Concurrency: cursor: pin S wait on X **time_waited_micro** | 1,241,241,858 |
| 48,148 | Concurrency: cursor: pin S wait on X **total_timeouts** | 0 |
| 48,148 | Concurrency: cursor: pin S wait on X **total_waits** | 4,849 |
| 48,149 | Concurrency: cursor: pin S wait on X **time_waited_micro** | 1,243,586,414 |
| 48,149 | Concurrency: cursor: pin S wait on X **total_timeouts** | 0 |
| 48,149 | Concurrency: cursor: pin S wait on X **total_waits** | 4,851 |

***Figure 3-5b.*** *DBA_HIST_SYSTEM_EVENT "normalized" to the key-value pair format*

Figure 3-6a shows the multicolumn table format of DBA_HIST_ IOSTAT_FUNCTION. A SQL "describe" can be used to see all the columns of DBA_HIST_ IOSTAT_FUNCTION. You may note that the values in the various columns are cumulative rather being the value for just that particular snap_id.

The source SQL to produce Figure 3-6a follows.

```
with iostat_function as
(
select * from dba_hist_iostat_function
)
select snap_id, function_name, small_read_megabytes, large_
read_megabytes
, number_of_waits, wait_time
from iostat_function
where function_name = 'Buffer Cache Reads'
order by snap_id
;
```

| SNAP_ID | FUNCTION_NAME | SMALL READ MEGA BYTES | LARGE READ MEGA BYTES | NUMBER OF WAITS | WAIT TIME |
|---|---|---|---|---|---|
| 48,148 | Buffer Cache Reads | 9,047,625 | 8,993,968 | 982,515,967 | 1,034,609,247 |
| 48,149 | Buffer Cache Reads | 9,051,196 | 8,995,110 | 982,864,806 | 1,034,880,013 |
| 48,150 | Buffer Cache Reads | 9,077,988 | 9,005,709 | 985,792,976 | 1,038,856,736 |
| 48,151 | Buffer Cache Reads | 9,082,404 | 9,009,933 | 986,269,790 | 1,039,265,591 |
| 48,152 | Buffer Cache Reads | 9,086,901 | 9,011,911 | 986,748,186 | 1,039,731,536 |
| 48,153 | Buffer Cache Reads | 9,090,460 | 9,021,225 | 987,112,353 | 1,040,426,769 |
| 48,154 | Buffer Cache Reads | 9,093,819 | 9,022,334 | 987,435,822 | 1,040,818,953 |
| 48,155 | Buffer Cache Reads | 9,097,183 | 9,023,952 | 987,786,473 | 1,041,010,331 |

***Figure 3-6a.*** *Multicolumn table format of DBA_HIST_IOSTAT_ FUNCTION*

Figure 3-6b shows DBA_HIST_IOSTAT_FUNCTION "normalized" to the key-value pair format. This is accomplished by concatenating the function name with each of the column names to form the metric name. The SQL source code to produce this figure follows.

```
with iostat_function as
(
select * from dba_hist_iostat_function
)
, unpivot_iostat_function as
(
      select a.snap_id, a.function_id metric_id, function_name
|| ' small_read_megabytes' metric_name, small_read_megabytes
cumulative_value , a.dbid, a.instance_number from iostat_function a
union select a.snap_id, a.function_id metric_id, function_name
|| ' small_write_megabytes' metric_name,  small_write_megabytes
cumulative_value , a.dbid, a.instance_number from iostat_function a
```

```
union select a.snap_id, a.function_id metric_id, function_name
|| ' large_read_megabytes' metric_name, large_read_megabytes
cumulative_value , a.dbid, a.instance_number from iostat_function a
union select a.snap_id, a.function_id metric_id, function_name
|| ' large_write_megabytes' metric_name, large_write_megabytes
cumulative_value , a.dbid, a.instance_number from iostat_function a
union select a.snap_id, a.function_id metric_id, function_name
|| ' small_read_reqs' metric_name, small_read_reqs cumulative_
value , a.dbid, a.instance_number from iostat_function a
union select a.snap_id, a.function_id metric_id, function_name
|| ' small_write_reqs' metric_name, small_write_reqs cumulative_
value , a.dbid, a.instance_number from iostat_function a
union select a.snap_id, a.function_id metric_id, function_name
|| ' large_read_reqs' metric_name, large_read_reqs cumulative_
value , a.dbid, a.instance_number from iostat_function a
union select a.snap_id, a.function_id metric_id, function_name
|| ' large_write_reqs' metric_name, large_write_reqs cumulative_
value , a.dbid, a.instance_number from iostat_function a
union select a.snap_id, a.function_id metric_id, function_name
|| ' number_of_waits' metric_name, number_of_waits cumulative_
value , a.dbid, a.instance_number from iostat_function a
union select a.snap_id, a.function_id metric_id, function_name
|| ' wait_time' metric_name, wait_time cumulative_value ,
a.dbid, a.instance_number from iostat_function a
)
select snap_id, metric_name, cumulative_value
from unpivot_iostat_function
where metric_name like '%Buffer Cache Reads%'
order by snap_id
;
```

| SNAP_ID | METRIC_NAME | CUMULATIVE_VALUE |
|---|---|---|
| 48,148 | Buffer Cache Reads **large_read_megabytes** | 8,993,968 |
| 48,148 | Buffer Cache Reads **large_read_reqs** | 10,083,438 |
| 48,148 | Buffer Cache Reads **large_write_megabytes** | 0 |
| 48,148 | Buffer Cache Reads **large_write_reqs** | 0 |
| 48,148 | Buffer Cache Reads **number_of_waits** | 982,515,967 |
| 48,148 | Buffer Cache Reads **small_read_megabytes** | 9,047,625 |
| 48,148 | Buffer Cache Reads **small_read_reqs** | 1,040,977,453 |
| 48,148 | Buffer Cache Reads **small_write_megabytes** | 0 |
| 48,148 | Buffer Cache Reads **small_write_reqs** | 0 |
| 48,148 | Buffer Cache Reads **wait_time** | 1,034,609,247 |
| 48,149 | Buffer Cache Reads **large_read_megabytes** | 8,995,110 |
| 48,149 | Buffer Cache Reads **large_read_reqs** | 10,084,863 |
| 48,149 | Buffer Cache Reads **large_write_megabytes** | 0 |
| 48,149 | Buffer Cache Reads **large_write_reqs** | 0 |
| 48,149 | Buffer Cache Reads **number_of_waits** | 982,864,806 |
| 48,149 | Buffer Cache Reads **small_read_megabytes** | 9,051,196 |
| 48,149 | Buffer Cache Reads **small_read_reqs** | 1,041,336,306 |
| 48,149 | Buffer Cache Reads **small_write_megabytes** | 0 |
| 48,149 | Buffer Cache Reads **small_write_reqs** | 0 |
| 48,149 | Buffer Cache Reads **wait_time** | 1,034,880,013 |

***Figure 3-6b.*** *DBA_HIST_IOSTAT_FUNCTION "normalized" to the key-value pair format*

The how-to for unpivoting the data to obtain a normalized structure is simple. I use a SQL statement to do this, taking advantage of the WITH clause subquery factoring capability of Oracle (example code snippet shown in the following text). When implemented, this SQL query will convert the columns of data into rows, with each row having a metric on the left and its value on the right. Following is an example code for normalizing data.

Figure 3-7 illustrates an example code for normalizing DBA_HIST_ SYSTEM_EVENT.

```
with system_event as
(
select * from dba_hist_system_event
)
, unpivot_system_event as
(
       select a.snap_id, a.event_id metric_id, wait_class || ': ' ||
event_name || ' total_waits' metric_name, total_waits cumulative_value
, a.dbid, a.instance_number from system_event a
union select a.snap_id, a.event_id metric_id, wait_class || ': ' ||
event_name || ' total_timeouts' metric_name,  total_timeouts
cumulative_value , a.dbid, a.instance_number from system_event a
union select a.snap_id, a.event_id metric_id, wait_class || ': ' ||
event_name || ' time_waited_micro' metric_name,  time_waited_micro
cumulative_value , a.dbid, a.instance_number from system_event a
)
select snap_id, metric_name, cumulative_value
from unpivot_system_event
where metric_name like '%cursor: pin S wait on X%'
order by 1,2
;
```

***Figure 3-7.*** *SQL code snippet for normalizing DBA_HIST_SYSTEM_ EVENT*

The reason I place a significant emphasis on normalizing data is that it is essential for enabling you to instrument large quantities of metrics. Since the motivation for building a better process is to obtain a more complete analysis, it's important to use all the metrics that might inform your analysis. Although the normalization process is essential, it is not complicated. In fact, it is very simple and easy to implement. Once you understand how to code to normalize data, the door opens for you to instrument any metric. Later in this chapter, I explain how to implement custom queries to enable you to use any data source.

Some metrics are already persisted in the key-value pair (KVP) format, so do not need to go through the normalization step. For example, those metrics found in DBA_HIST_SYS_TIME_MODEL, %OSSTAT, %SYSMETRIC_SUMMARY, and %SYSSTAT already use the KVP format.

As you can see, the key-value pair data structure can easily be implemented in a relational database. It is regularly used by computer scientists, and I have made use of it many times over the years. The usefulness of this structure can be inferred from its ever-increasing use in the field of analytics. Many recently developed systems/tools use this format instead of a more traditional structure including NoSQL, MongoDB, Redis, JSON, and XML. I expect this list will grow as developers comprehend and take hold of the power of big data techniques.

# Convert to Delta Values

Let's say, for example, you had a calorie monitor that measured your cumulative calorie usage and reported this every hour. In a certain use case, that would be an important metric; however, you would probably also want to know how many calories you used in a particular hour (i.e., the "delta value"). In the case of Oracle performance metrics, Oracle provides many of the metrics as cumulative values, but we usually want to know the "delta value," that is, the value for that metric in a particular AWR snapshot period (usually one hour). So, to make the metric more useful, I convert the cumulative values to delta values.

For the purposes of the DOPA process, there are some metrics which are already expressed as delta values; in these cases the values given represent an average of the measurements taken during that time interval (i.e., the snapshot interval). Oracle's AWR data set includes many metrics that fit into this category. *Response Time Per Txn* is one example. As per the following details, this metric shows the average response time per transaction in centiseconds per transaction for all the transactions occurring in a one-hour interval. [Actually, the AWR snapshot interval duration depends on how your AWR snapshotting is set up; the interval duration is by default one hour, while much less common, I've seen some use 15- or 30-minute intervals. Shorter AWR snapshot intervals provide for more fine-grained metric values.]

- DBA_HIST_SYSMETRIC_SUMMARY.METRIC_NAME = "Response Time Per Txn"

- Example average value: 220 centiseconds per Txn

- Average value is for the interval marked by

  - BEGIN_TIME: 5/15/2018 01:00:00

  - END_TIME: 5/15/2018 02:00:00

However, for a certain set of metrics which Oracle refers to as statistics, a cumulative value since instance start-up is given at each interval. The values for these metrics increase over time. The metrics persisted in DBA_HIST_SYS_TIME_MODEL, %SYSSTAT, %OSSTAT, %LATCH, %SYSTEM_EVENT, and %IOSTAT_FUNCTION are examples of this type of metric. A close examination of the data in the listings in Figures 3-4, 3-5, and 3-6 also shows the cumulative nature of the values collected by Oracle for the metric. Data that is presented as a cumulative value requires some manipulation in order to be used in the DOPA process for analysis.

The manipulation I do involves converting the cumulative data into deltas. Logically, this makes sense because what we are concerned with for performance issues is the change from one interval to the next as opposed to the cumulative value since instance start-up. So in this step, I'm preparing the data to show the values for the metric in that single snapshot interval (i.e., the "delta") rather than the cumulative value which is recorded by Oracle. These deltas can be calculated using Oracle's LAG function [for more details on the LAG function, refer to the Oracle documentation; see the following text for an example of LAG in this context].

Figure 3-8 shows an example of using the LAG function convert raw data that is cumulative in nature to deltas.

The example SQL code for this follows:

```
select snap_id
, 'dba_hist_sysstat' metric_source
, stat_name metric_name
, value cumulative_value
, value - lag(value) over (order by snap_id) delta_value
from dba_hist_sysstat a natural join dba_hist_snapshot
where 1=1
  -- example looking ot only one metric/statistic
  and stat_name = 'user I/O wait time'
order by snap_id
;
```

| SNAP_ID | METRIC_SOURCE | METRIC_NAME | CUMULATIVE VALUE | DELTA VALUE |
|--------:|---------------|-------------|-----------------:|------------:|
| 20,239 | dba_hist_sysstat | user I/O wait time | 202,531,646 | 379,566 |
| 20,240 | dba_hist_sysstat | user I/O wait time | 203,184,089 | 652,443 |
| 20,241 | dba_hist_sysstat | user I/O wait time | 206,150,411 | 2,966,322 |
| 20,242 | dba_hist_sysstat | user I/O wait time | 208,235,826 | 2,085,415 |
| 20,243 | dba_hist_sysstat | user I/O wait time | 209,548,656 | 1,312,830 |
| 20,244 | dba_hist_sysstat | user I/O wait time | 209,870,279 | 321,623 |
| 20,245 | dba_hist_sysstat | user I/O wait time | 210,576,986 | 706,707 |
| 20,246 | dba_hist_sysstat | user I/O wait time | 211,229,403 | 652,417 |
| 20,247 | dba_hist_sysstat | user I/O wait time | 211,778,376 | 548,973 |
| 20,248 | dba_hist_sysstat | user I/O wait time | 212,205,075 | 426,699 |

***Figure 3-8.*** *Example SQL code using Oracle's LAG analytic function to convert metric values that are cumulative in nature to the delta value for that interval. This is a crucial step in the data preparation stage.*

# Union Data from All Sources

Once I have the normalized key-value pair format of the metrics from
several different sources, I union them together to form one big virtual
data set.

Figure 3-9 shows an example of normalized data that has been
unioned for analysis.

Example source SQL for unioning the metrics is too big to include in
the text of the book so it is provided as a file: DOPA_Normalized_Unioned_
Metrics_3_9.sql.

| SNAP_ID | STAT_SOURCE | METRIC_NAME | AVERAGE |
|---|---|---|---|
| 20,246 | dba_hist_iostat_function | Buffer Cache Reads large_read_megabytes | 3,435 |
| 20,246 | dba_hist_iostat_function | Buffer Cache Reads large_read_reqs | 3,793 |
| 20,246 | dba_hist_iostat_function | Buffer Cache Reads large_write_megabytes | 0 |
| 20,246 | dba_hist_iostat_function | Buffer Cache Reads large_write_reqs | 0 |
| 20,246 | dba_hist_iostat_function | Buffer Cache Reads number_of_waits | 2,900,560 |
| 20,246 | dba_hist_iostat_function | Buffer Cache Reads small_read_megabytes | 46,643 |
| 20,246 | dba_hist_iostat_function | Buffer Cache Reads small_read_reqs | 2,980,290 |
| 20,246 | dba_hist_iostat_function | Buffer Cache Reads small_write_megabytes | 0 |
| 20,246 | dba_hist_iostat_function | Buffer Cache Reads small_write_reqs | 0 |
| 20,246 | dba_hist_iostat_function | Buffer Cache Reads wait_time | 6,000,190 |
| 20,246 | dba_hist_latch | 1: cache buffers chains gets | 80,497,776 |
| 20,246 | dba_hist_latch | 1: cache buffers chains immediate_gets | 3,544,493 |
| 20,246 | dba_hist_latch | 1: cache buffers chains immediate_misses | 129 |
| 20,246 | dba_hist_latch | 1: cache buffers chains misses | 8,611 |
| 20,246 | dba_hist_latch | 1: cache buffers chains sleep1 | 0 |
| 20,246 | dba_hist_latch | 1: cache buffers chains sleep2 | 0 |
| 20,246 | dba_hist_latch | 1: cache buffers chains sleep3 | 0 |
| 20,246 | dba_hist_latch | 1: cache buffers chains sleep4 | 0 |
| 20,246 | dba_hist_latch | 1: cache buffers chains sleeps | 1,373 |
| 20,246 | dba_hist_latch | 1: cache buffers chains spin_gets | 7,566 |
| 20,246 | dba_hist_latch | 1: cache buffers chains wait_time | 47,864 |
| 20,246 | dba_hist_system_event | Concurrency: cursor: pin S wait on X time_waite | 25,000,397 |
| 20,246 | dba_hist_system_event | Concurrency: cursor: pin S wait on X total_timeo | 0 |
| 20,246 | dba_hist_system_event | Concurrency: cursor: pin S wait on X total_waits | 226 |
| 20,246 | dba_hist_system_event | Concurrency: latch: cache buffers chains time_w | 47,864 |
| 20,246 | dba_hist_system_event | Concurrency: latch: cache buffers chains total_ti | 0 |
| 20,246 | dba_hist_system_event | Concurrency: latch: cache buffers chains total_w | 1,047 |

***Figure 3-9.*** *Example set of normalized metrics unioned together and
ready for statistical analysis*

The union of the normalized metrics is what allows me to scale my analysis to include the thousands of the metrics available. Once the data is unioned, it is a simple task to tell the "machine" to apply the same analysis to all the KVP rows.

Up to this point, I have not moved any data, but the data is perceived logically by the Oracle query engine as one giant metric table. I can continue to add metrics. Since operations on the data are being performed inside the database and data is not being moved around, it is not a resource-consuming process. Even with the thousands of metrics I've implemented so far, I have not come close to hitting the machine's capacity limits. The analysis I run using data from the seven tables I have implemented so far includes 2 million rows of metrics and takes approximately 30 secs to 2 ½ mins. Theoretically, at least, you should be able to add all the metrics you want without encountering difficulties.

## Custom Queries

As mentioned above, you are not limited to the data collected by AWR for your analysis. You can use the basic process I have explained to capture data from any source that can be formatted as a time-series KVP metric. A custom query will enable you to instrument data retrieved from sources such as dba_advisor tables and active session history results, as well as many other sources.

For example, you could use this process to instrument *log file switching* which is a time-based metric persisted in v$log_history. You would begin by "unpivoting" this data.

A simple query as follows could be a starting point for the unpivot code:

```
-- Log File switches - Grouped by hour
SELECT to_char(trunc(first_time, 'HH24'),'YYYY-MM-DD HH24:MI') "Date"
, count(1) "Total LFS per hour"
FROM v$log_history
where trunc(first_time) > = trunc(sysdate-14)
GROUP by to_char(trunc(first_time, 'HH24'),'YYYY-MM-DD HH24:MI')
order by to_date(to_char(trunc(first_time, 'HH24'),'YYYY-MM-DD
HH24:MI'), 'YYYY-MM-DD HH24:MI') desc
;
```

Figure 3-10 shows an example what the log file data would look like once the above SQL code is run—tall and skinny, but not yet a KVP.

| Date | Total LFS per hour |
|------|--------------------|
| 2018-05-22 22:00 | 2 |
| 2018-05-22 21:00 | 2 |
| 2018-05-22 20:00 | 2 |
| 2018-05-22 19:00 | 2 |
| 2018-05-22 18:00 | 2 |
| 2018-05-22 17:00 | 2 |
| 2018-05-22 16:00 | 2 |
| 2018-05-22 15:00 | 2 |
| 2018-05-22 14:00 | 2 |
| 2018-05-22 13:00 | 2 |
| 2018-05-22 12:00 | 2 |
| 2018-05-22 11:00 | 2 |
| 2018-05-22 10:00 | 4 |
| 2018-05-22 09:00 | 2 |
| 2018-05-22 08:00 | 2 |
| 2018-05-22 07:00 | 2 |
| 2018-05-22 06:00 | 2 |
| 2018-05-22 05:00 | 2 |
| 2018-05-22 04:00 | 2 |
| 2018-05-22 03:00 | 2 |

***Figure 3-10.*** *Example log file data that can easily be normalized into the KVP structure*

The last step would be to normalize this table into the standard KVP format, with a column for time, a column for metric name (log file switches per hour), and a third column for value.

Figure 3-11 shows v$log_history in key-value pair format. I've joined v$log_history with DBA_HIST_SNAPSHOT (matching the time values) so that I can get the snap_ids just like all the AWR metrics have. To use this in the DOPA process, one would just need to union this in with the other metrics using the same method being used for normal AWR metrics.

Example SQL code for converting v$log_history to a key-value pair metric.

```
-- Log File switches - Grouped by hour
-- converted to Key-Value-Pair metric
with log_history as
( select to_char(trunc(first_time, 'HH24'),'YYYY-MM-DD HH24:MI') "Date"
, count(1) "Total LFS per hour"
FROM v$log_history
where trunc(first_time) > = trunc(sysdate-14)
GROUP by to_char(first_time, 'Dy'), to_char(trunc(first_time,
'HH24'),'YYYY-MM-DD HH24:MI')
order by to_date(to_char(trunc(first_time, 'HH24'),'YYYY-MM-DD
HH24:MI'), 'YYYY-MM-DD HH24:MI') desc
)
, log_history_normalized as
(
select snap_id, 'v$log_history' metric_source
, 'Total LFS per hour' metric_name
, "Total LFS per hour" delta_value
from log_history lh
, dba_hist_snapshot snap
where lh."Date" = to_char(trunc(snap.begin_interval_time,
'HH24'),'YYYY-MM-DD HH24:MI')
)
```

```
select snap_id, metric_source, metric_name, delta_value
from log_history_normalized
where 1=1
order by snap_id
;
```

| SNAP_ID | METRIC_SOURCE | METRIC_NAME | DELTA VALUE |
|---|---|---|---|
| 20,240 | v$log_history | Total LFS per hour | 18 |
| 20,241 | v$log_history | Total LFS per hour | 10 |
| 20,242 | v$log_history | Total LFS per hour | 47 |
| 20,243 | v$log_history | Total LFS per hour | 4 |
| 20,244 | v$log_history | Total LFS per hour | 4 |
| 20,245 | v$log_history | Total LFS per hour | 2 |
| 20,246 | v$log_history | Total LFS per hour | 2 |
| 20,247 | v$log_history | Total LFS per hour | 2 |
| 20,248 | v$log_history | Total LFS per hour | 2 |
| 20,249 | v$log_history | Total LFS per hour | 2 |
| 20,250 | v$log_history | Total LFS per hour | 2 |

*Figure 3-11.*  *Example output with v$log_history converted to a key-value pair metric*

Not all metrics have a data pattern that make it easy to convert to the KVP format. Histograms are a data source that I would put in this category. I have not spent time to discover a method for implementing this type of data, but I am sure there is a way. I welcome any input from others who have a desire to work on this particular aspect.

# Summary

Hopefully, this discussion has enabled you to understand the usefulness of adopting the KVP/normalized data structure. Data prep is an easy step, more or less a housekeeping step, but it is essential for scalability. Only when the data is formatted into a single, large, virtual data set does it become possible to include the vast quantity of data that we want to include in the analysis. Normalized data can be manipulated with a single SQL statement in situ, and therefore it is possible to include a vast number of metrics. It is the quantity of metrics that assures us that our analysis is fully informed and therefore accurate.

This discussion should also have convinced you that the process of converting MCT structures to this normalized structure is easily accomplished. Normalization is accomplished using SQL, the language of the database. It is a language we are all familiar with and use every day.

The code snippets I've included will provide the example you need to be able to select and implement your own set of metrics. Your choice of metrics will depend on your organization's goals and objectives.

I listed in the preceding text the metrics I have included to date. I plan to continue to add metrics as I am able because I believe having more metrics adds depth of understanding. My goal is to instrument every source of metrics that could be useful for performance tuning; any metric stored within Oracle is a potential candidate. Of course, adding metrics takes time, so I will prioritize.

Oracle continues to add new features to their product. Each time they do, they add a metric by which its performance can be measured. The analysis I perform with the metrics I have implemented to date takes approximately one minute to run. With this analysis, I have not come anywhere close to maximizing the machine's capability. Theoretically, it should be possible to include all of the metrics in the analysis, but I don't know yet if this is true. I also don't know if it is necessary. I am still in the discovery phase.

When using a traditional approach, it had always plagued me that my finite ability to process information was necessarily forcing me to limit my analysis to a few select metrics and ignore so many others. I believed I must be missing out on some valuable information. With the DOPA process, the machine is doing the analysis and pulling out for my attention only the metrics most likely to predict a problem, so the number of metrics that can be included in the analysis is vastly expanded while the speed and accuracy of the analysis enhanced.

The next chapter will discuss the first part of that analysis, statistical analysis.

# CHAPTER 4

# Statistical Analysis

This chapter addresses the statistical manipulation of the data that has been collected and formatted. I'll start by reviewing some basic statistical concepts, including normal ranges, outliers, and variance, and then discuss how these concepts are applied as part of the DOPA process to establish normal ranges for the host of metrics that don't have well-known norms. Don't worry, you don't have to break out the statistics books; I will show you how to use the embedded Oracle functions to easily accomplish this statistical analysis.

So far, you have learned how to gather the data, unpivot/normalize the values into key-value pairs, and union them together to create a single virtual data set of metrics and their values. The next step in the DOPA process is to perform some basic statistical operations. Once performed, these statistical calculations will allow the program to identify which part(s) of the database are experiencing performance problems by flagging those that are "abnormal" based on the statistical analysis.

For some metrics collected by Oracle, there are absolute values which can be identified as "normal." When these metrics exceed the "normal" values, a problem is clearly indicated. For example, a DBA will most likely be familiar with the following metrics and have some idea about the expected values for them (I've included some of the numbers that I consider normal):

> Host CPU Utilization (%): optimal response time no
> greater than 65%

© Roger Cornejo 2018
R. Cornejo, *Dynamic Oracle Performance Analytics*,
https://doi.org/10.1007/978-1-4842-4137-0_4

Average Active Sessions: less than or equal to CPU count

Average Synchronous Single-Block Read Latency: no greater than 20 milliseconds

Run Queue Per Sec: I am concerned with values above 5

Database Wait Time Ratio: no greater than 80%

DB time

User I/O wait time

Session Limit %

While it's true that some of the metrics have a known expected value, in my experience the metrics with known values are the exception rather than the rule (given the thousands of metrics available in the AWR). The vast majority of metric values contained in Oracle's repository do not have a known absolute normal value. That might be because the DBA is unfamiliar with the metrics, or they might be measurements of things that vary widely from machine to machine and even from time to time, depending on the workload, the number and types of applications running, the number of users, etc., and hence what is "normal" for one machine at a given time may change with changing use.

Following are some examples of metrics for which a DBA will probably not know "normal" values:

Response Time Per Txn

User Transaction Per Sec

Redo Generated Per Sec

Network Traffic Volume Per Sec

Physical Read Total Bytes Per Sec

Physical Write Total IO Requests Per Sec

Current Open Cursors Count

redo log space requests

hard parse elapsed time

parse time elapsed

Given that it is humanly impossible to know or calculate manually the normal ranges for the many thousands of metrics available to us in the AWR, I have devised a method which uses simple statistical functions built into Oracle to compute the normal ranges for each metric. Again, the reason for this is so that the program can identify metrics as problematic when they exceed the normal value established by that statistical analysis.

Most computer professionals will have had at least some basic statistics as part of their schooling and will therefore be somewhat familiar with the statistical concepts of norms and standard deviations, but I'm going to do a quick review before proceeding just for clarity. I'll define a few terms and then explain how they are used in the DOPA process.

# Statistics Review

**Mean** is the average of a set of numbers calculated by taking the sum of the numbers and then dividing by the quantity of numbers considered. Figure 4-1 shows the mathematical computation of the mean for five numbers, and immediately following it in Figure 4-2, you will see how to accomplish this computation using Oracle's embedded function.

$$\frac{(7 + 2 + 10 + 4 + 12)}{5} = 7$$

***Figure 4-1.*** *This is the mathematical computation of mean for the five numbers: 7, 2, 10, 4, and 12*

Given a table of values (7, 2, 10, 4, and 12), you can use Oracle's embedded functions to calculate mean (average) as follows:

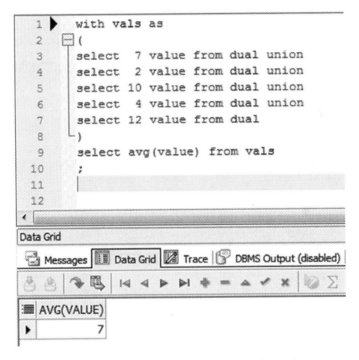

***Figure 4-2.*** *This is an example code to accomplish the computation of mean using Oracle's embedded function*

**Variance** is a statistical term that expresses how widely dispersed the data points in a particular set are. In a data set with high variance, the data points will be spread out more than in a data set with low variance. The mathematical formula for calculating sample variance used by Oracle is shown in Figure 4-3, and sample code for calculating the same using Oracle's embedded functions is given in Figure 4-4.

$$s^2 = \frac{\sum_{i=1}^{n}\left(X_i - X_{avg}\right)^2}{n-1}$$

***Figure 4-3.*** *This is the mathematical formula for calculating sample variance*

# Calculating the Sample Variance Using the Oracle Function

Given the same table of values as in the mean example in the preceding section, an example of the variance calculation in Oracle follows:

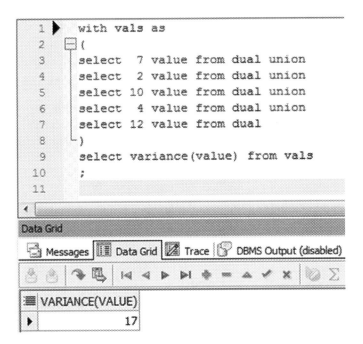

***Figure 4-4.*** *This is a sample code to calculate variance using Oracle's embedded functions*

**Standard deviation** is another way of expressing the degree of dispersion of data points in a particular set. The formula for its calculation is shown in Figure 4-5. As you can see from the formula, it is simply the square root of variance. Figure 4-6 shows how to accomplish this calculation using Oracle's embedded functions. As with variance, when standard deviation is low, it indicates that values are grouped close to the mean, and when standard deviation is high, it indicates that the values are much more widely dispersed. Either calculation can be used to help improve understanding of a particular data set. The main difference between the two is that while variance is expressed as squared units, standard deviation is expressed in the same values as the mean of the data set. For this reason, I have chosen to use standard deviation in my calculations.

$$\sigma = \sqrt{\frac{\sum_{i=1}^{n}(X_i - X_{avg})^2}{n - 1}}$$

**Figure 4-5.** *Mathematical calculation of standard deviation*

Given the same table of values as in the mean example in the above section, an example of the standard deviation calculation in Oracle follows:

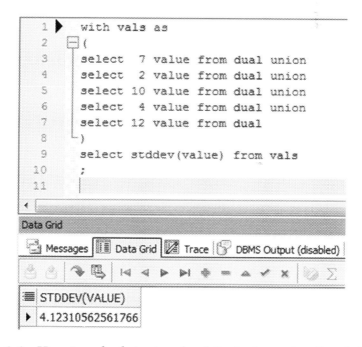

**Figure 4-6.** *How to calculate standard deviation using Oracle's embedded functions*

Without going too deep, statisticians have adopted a theorem called the **central limit theorem** which enables us to assume that the sample mean of a set of random variables will tend toward a normal distribution, which enables us to compare means of different samples. Furthermore, the three-sigma rule (empirical rule) states that in a **normal distribution**, most of the data will fall within three standard distributions of the mean and, more specifically, that it will fall into a pattern as follows:

> 68% will be within the first standard deviation from the mean.
>
> 95% within two standard deviations.
>
> 99.7% within three standard deviations.

Normal distributions are often represented graphically and can be recognized as the familiar bell curve represented in Figure 4-7.

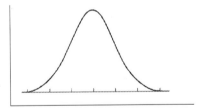

***Figure 4-7.***  *This is a figure of a bell curve showing a normal distribution*

One last concept that is important to understand is outliers. Outliers are data points that are very far from most of the other data points in a set of data. Figure 4-8 shows a set of values for Average Synchronous Single-Block Read Latency on an hourly basis. It is clear to see from the graph that the value for the 10:00 hour is an outlier since it is so far beyond the other values.

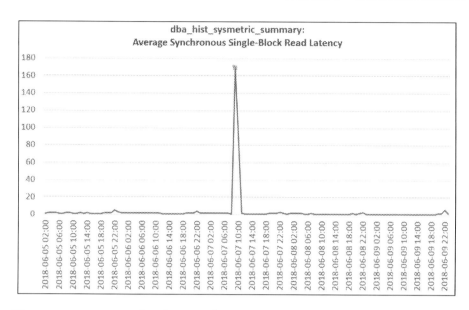

**Figure 4-8.** *Example of an outlier in the data that one would want to remove before calculating the normal range*

Removing outliers is important because they can significantly skew the calculation of "normal" for a given set of data. We want to identify them and remove them prior to calculating normal ranges for this reason.

A common method for identifying outliers uses a concept called the interquartile range or IQR. This method divides the data into quartiles by calculating the median of the numbers in the lower half of the data set (called Q1) and the median of the numbers in the upper half of the data set (called Q3). The data points contained between Q1 and Q3 represent the middle 50% of the data. A number is considered to be an outlier if it is more than 1.5 times the IQR below Q1 or 1.5 times the IQR above Q3.

# Statistics in the DOPA Process

Having laid a foundation of basic statistical analysis, I will now proceed to show you how I use statistics in the DOPA process to establish "normal values" for a given metric.

When a problem is reported, I collect the metric data for the week prior. One week has been my default time frame, because on most of the databases on which I work, this is the AWR retention setting. For establishing normal ranges, I want to consider metrics that reflect normal operation of the database, so I use metric values from a time interval when it was performing without problems. For example, if the problem occurred today, I would grab the data from the previous week and include all the metrics except those collected over the last 24 hours when the problem occurred. The AWR retention setting can be altered and it is probably useful to do so; I have been attempting to increase retention to 30 days on our databases so that a longer pre-problem comparative block of data is available for reference and establishing normal values.

Once I have my metric data for what I believe is a pre-problem time interval long enough to be representative of normal function, I begin my statistical manipulation by identifying outliers. I use the IQR method that identifies numbers more than 1.5 interquartile ranges (IQRs) above Q3 and more than 1.5 IQRs below Q1 as outliers. I have instrumented the multiplication factor as a variable since there may be instances when I want to exclude or include more numbers at the extreme, but I use 1.5 as my default. An example of code used to calculate the IQR for use in identifying outliers is shown in Figure 4-9.

```
-- example outlier removal code using the IQR method
with vals as
(
select snap_id
, 'dba_hist_sysmetric_summary' metric_source
, metric_name, average metric_value
from dba_hist_sysmetric_summary
where metric_name like nvl(:metric_name, 'Enqueue Requests Per Txn')
/* other metrics in dba_hist_sysmetric_summary include
Average Active Sessions
Average Synchronous Single-Block Read Latency
*/
)
, iqr as
(
select stat.*
, Percentile_Cont(0.25) WITHIN GROUP(Order By metric_value) OVER() As
Q1
, Percentile_Cont(0.75) WITHIN GROUP(Order By metric_value) OVER() As
Q3
, Percentile_Cont(0.75) WITHIN GROUP(Order By metric_value) OVER()
- Percentile_Cont(0.25) WITHIN GROUP(Order By metric_value) OVER() as
IQR
from vals stat
)
, outliers as
( select iqr.*
, case when Q1 - (1.5 * IQR) >0 then Q1 - (1.5 * IQR) else 0 end as
lower_outlier
, Q3 + (1.5 * IQR) as upper_outlier
from iqr
)
select snap_id, metric_name
, metric_Value
, q1
, q3
, iqr
, lower_outlier
, upper_outlier
, case when metric_value > upper_outlier then 'OUTLIER (high)'
      when metric_Value < lower_outlier then 'OUTLIER (low)'
      else 'not an outlier' end outlier_note
from outliers
order by snap_id
;
```

***Figure 4-9.*** *This figure shows code used for removing outliers*

When the code in Figure 4-9 is executed for a particular database for a particular time interval, the result will be a table. The bind variable for metric_name can be left blank to default to "Enqueue Requests Per Txn"; otherwise provide another metric_name from dba_hist_sysmetric_ summary. The result table is shown in Figure 4-10. In this table, you can see the metric name and its value for each interval. Q1 and Q3 are the same for each and have been used to establish the upper and lower bounds for determining outliers. If the metric value for a given instance is determined to be an outlier, this is indicated in the "outlier" column as well as whether it is an upper or lower outlier.

| SNAP_ID | METRIC_NAME | METRIC VALUE | Q1 | Q3 | IQR | LOWER OUTLIER | UPPER OUTLIER | OUTLIER_NOTE |
|---|---|---|---|---|---|---|---|---|
| 81,122 | Enqueue Requests Per Txn | 101 | 53 | 94 | 41 | 0 | 156 | not an outlier |
| 81,123 | Enqueue Requests Per Txn | 87 | 53 | 94 | 41 | 0 | 156 | not an outlier |
| 81,124 | Enqueue Requests Per Txn | 157 | 53 | 94 | 41 | 0 | 156 | OUTLIER (high) |
| 81,125 | Enqueue Requests Per Txn | 135 | 53 | 94 | 41 | 0 | 156 | not an outlier |
| 81,126 | Enqueue Requests Per Txn | 178 | 53 | 94 | 41 | 0 | 156 | OUTLIER (high) |
| 81,127 | Enqueue Requests Per Txn | 124 | 53 | 94 | 41 | 0 | 156 | not an outlier |
| 81,128 | Enqueue Requests Per Txn | 155 | 53 | 94 | 41 | 0 | 156 | not an outlier |
| 81,129 | Enqueue Requests Per Txn | 135 | 53 | 94 | 41 | 0 | 156 | not an outlier |
| 81,130 | Enqueue Requests Per Txn | 94 | 53 | 94 | 41 | 0 | 156 | not an outlier |
| 81,131 | Enqueue Requests Per Txn | 95 | 53 | 94 | 41 | 0 | 156 | not an outlier |
| 81,132 | Enqueue Requests Per Txn | 86 | 53 | 94 | 41 | 0 | 156 | not an outlier |
| 81,133 | Enqueue Requests Per Txn | 53 | 53 | 94 | 41 | 0 | 156 | not an outlier |
| 81,134 | Enqueue Requests Per Txn | 66 | 53 | 94 | 41 | 0 | 156 | not an outlier |
| 81,135 | Enqueue Requests Per Txn | 77 | 53 | 94 | 41 | 0 | 156 | not an outlier |
| 81,136 | Enqueue Requests Per Txn | 1,144 | 53 | 94 | 41 | 0 | 156 | OUTLIER (high) |
| 81,137 | Enqueue Requests Per Txn | 156 | 53 | 94 | 41 | 0 | 156 | not an outlier |
| 81,138 | Enqueue Requests Per Txn | 88 | 53 | 94 | 41 | 0 | 156 | not an outlier |

**Figure 4-10.**  *This table represents the result for the code shown in Figure 4-9 executed for a particular database for a particular time interval and shows Q1 and Q3 and whether the value was determined to be an outlier*

The following example demonstrates why removing outliers is important. Figure 4-11 shows the data points for *single-block read latency* values over an eight-day time period.

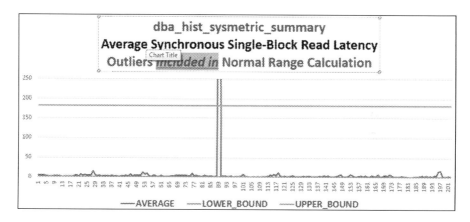

**Figure 4-11.** *Single high value for single-block read latency over approximately an eight-day collection interval*

In this graph, you will observe a single peak where the value is much higher for a single time interval than all the values for the other time intervals. The value was 1230 during that hour. I would normally expect single-block read latency to be less than 10 milliseconds. The abnormally high value occurred only once and there were no user complaints related to it, so I assumed it was a glitch in the data collection. If the 1230 value is included in the calculation of mean, it significantly skews the results. Including the high value yields a normal range with upper bound of 182 milliseconds. This upper bound is represented graphically by the gray horizontal line at 182 in Figure 4-11. Remembering that we should expect single-block latency to be under 10, using this upper bound would cause the program to fail to identify many abnormal values.

When the extremely high value is excluded as an outlier, the calculated mean value is 8 milliseconds. This is a much more accurate calculation for an upper bound for this metric. Figure 4-12 shows the values for upper bound before removing outliers and after outliers are removed.

Average Synchronous Single-Block Read Latency during a single hour interval  = 1230
Falsely elevates the NR upper bound to ~182 milliseconds
real NR upper bound ~8 milliseconds

***Figure 4-12.*** *Calculation of the upper bound when including the unusually high value and also when it is excluded as an outlier*

The graph for the data set when the outlier is removed is shown in Figure 4-13. Now that the outlier has been removed, the upper bound is determined to be 8, again represented by a horizontal gray line. Note that with this new upper bound, there are several metric values that rise above that line and will therefore be "flagged" as unusually high.

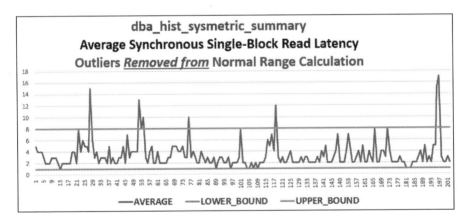

***Figure 4-13.*** *This graph shows the same data set as in the preceding figure after the outlier is removed. Note the new upper bound at 8.*

The interquartile range method for eliminating outliers is easy to implement using SQL and Oracle functions, and it has worked well for me thus far. I am not a statistician, so I am open to exploring alternate methods for removing outliers. The important point is that outliers should be removed prior to performing the next series of operations to ensure that real problems are not missed due to skewed results.

After I have removed outliers, I proceed to calculate the normal range for the remaining values. This is easily accomplished using two Oracle functions—MEAN and STDDEV. As the name implies, MEAN determines the arithmetic mean for the entire data set. STDDEV computes the standard deviation based on that mean and the existing data points.

I use the standard deviation to set the upper and lower bounds of the "normal range" of values for each metric. The upper bound of "normal" for each metric is established as 2 standard deviations above the mean and the lower bound is 2 standard deviations below the mean. This is fairly standard and is referred to as the range rule of thumb.

Once a normal range is established, individual values can be compared to the norm to determine if they are "abnormal." Examples of how *normal range* is used abound. Blood chemistry labs are one familiar usage. Based on samples from a very large patient population, a range of normal values has been established for various blood chemistry metrics, among them red blood cell (RBC) count. If you have labs drawn, you will usually see your individual test result listed alongside the range of normal. Figure 4-14 shows an example of test results for an individual's RBC. In this example the test results would be considered abnormal since the test result falls below the low end of the normal range.

| Test Completed | Result | Range* |
|---|---|---|
| Red Blood Cell Count | 4.2 million/ul | 4.7 to 6.1 million/ul |

*Figure 4-14.* *A common use of normal range is red blood cell count. This figure shows an example of the results of an individual test next to a normal range of values for that test.*

In addition to calculating the standard deviation, I also calculate the variance. As mentioned in the earlier review of statistics, both standard deviation and variance indicate the amount of variability in the data, the main difference being in the units themselves. I have found it most useful to look at standard deviation because it is in the same units as the metric themselves. However, if you are just trying to get an idea of which variables are the most widely ranging, looking at the variance might be more insightful. Because variance is a squared value, it will get larger more quickly and hence be more obvious.

Figure 4-15 shows an example of several CPU-related metrics and the results of the statistical analysis that has been performed on those metrics in order to prepare the data for the next step in the DOPA process.

| STAT_SOURCE | METRIC_NAME | LOWER_BOUND | AVERAGE_VALUE | UPPER BOUND |
|---|---|---|---|---|
| dba_hist_sys_time_model | background cpu time | 88,552,680 | 230,492,082 | 585,636,320 |
| dba_hist_sysmetric_summary | Background CPU Usage Per Sec | 2 | 6 | 16 |
| dba_hist_sysmetric_summary | CPU Usage Per Sec | 517 | 944 | 1,371 |
| dba_hist_sysmetric_summary | CPU Usage Per Txn | 339 | 427 | 497 |
| dba_hist_sysstat | CPU used by this session | 580,658 | 1,304,037 | 2,901,427 |
| dba_hist_sysstat | CPU used when call started | 163,310 | 546,551 | 1,565,198 |
| dba_hist_sysmetric_summary | Database CPU Time Ratio | 78 | 89 | 97 |
| dba_hist_sys_time_model | DB CPU | 18,743,951,677 | 33,989,028,752 | 49,234,105,827 |
| dba_hist_sysmetric_summary | Host CPU Usage Per Sec | 774 | 1,260 | 1,746 |
| dba_hist_sysmetric_summary | Host CPU Utilization (%) | 3 | 5 | 7 |
| dba_hist_osstat | OS_CPU_WAIT_TIME | 17,456 | 45,833 | 74,210 |
| dba_hist_sysstat | parse time cpu | 3,233 | 26,378 | 50,335 |
| dba_hist_sysstat | recursive cpu usage | 433,878 | 1,211,768 | 3,007,416 |
| dba_hist_sys_time_model | RMAN cpu time (backup/restore) | 20,636,685 | 90,951,512 | 228,423,925 |
| dba_hist_osstat | RSRC_MGR_CPU_WAIT_TIME | 1 | 344 | 708 |

***Figure 4-15.*** *This table displays several metrics with the results of the statistical analysis performed. The average, variance, standard deviation, and upper and lower bounds of the normal range are all given in columnar format.*

# Summary

This statistical analysis detailed in this chapter enables us to state with a good deal of certainty what is normal for any given metric. To summarize, the outliers have been removed and the mean has been established for the remaining data points. Using the calculated mean, the standard deviation and variance have been established. All of this calculation is accomplished using Oracle's embedded functions. This process of statistical manipulation is absolutely essential for the next step in the DOPA process, feature selection or flagging, which enables us to identify the metrics that are abnormal and, therefore, highly predictive of problems.

Next, we move on to feature selection.

# CHAPTER 5

# Feature Selection

In the last chapter, we discussed the statistical calculations necessary for establishing values that could be considered normal for a given metric. Once a normal is established for each metric, it is possible to identify metrics outside of normal and highlight them. These "abnormal" metrics are the ones that will be most useful for predicting the cause of performance issues in the database. In this chapter, I'll discuss the process of drawing out the Oracle performance metrics that are abnormal and therefore important for our analysis and discerning which ones can be safely ignored using a process that eliminates personal bias.

Sidebar Note:

For a simple example of feature selection in, say, the field of clinical blood chemistry analysis, consider that there could be hundreds of metrics for a single blood sample; feature selection as I'm using it here would provide a report where those metrics which fall outside of normal range are highlighted. The flagging of the out-of-normal blood chemistry results does not direct the physician as the clinical interpretation of, say, a low value for "red blood cell count" or that metric combined with low values for "hemoglobin," it simply saves the domain expert time in zeroing in on the metrics which are likely to be important to a diagnosis.

In the field of analytics, each instance is called a "feature," and "feature selection" refers to the process of identifying which features are most useful for creating a predictive model. Feature selection seeks to reduce the number of variables considered by excluding those that do not improve the accuracy of the model. Obviously, in order to do this, it must have a method for determining which variables are predictive.

For our use in performance tuning, an instance or feature is a metric value, and "feature selection" refers to the process of discovering which metrics are most likely causally related to a reported performance issue. Feature selection will highlight the metrics that are unusual (either lower or more commonly higher than normal) and therefore most likely to inform the tuning expert about the area of tuning that will yield the most significant improvement in performance. Accurate feature selection will produce a predictive model that is highly accurate. It is important to remember that the goal here is to produce a predictive model. The tuner will still be required to use his knowledge of the database and his skill to complete the analysis and perform the tuning, but by using the feature selection methods implemented as part of the DOPA process, he will be able to eliminate many variables not likely to yield significant performance improvement based on a scientific process, not based on personal bias or his familiarity/comfort with a given metric.

There are many methods for accomplishing feature selection. For example, machine learning methods use training sets of known problems to discover patterns that can be used to identify problems in other performance issues where the problem is not known. Other methods involve complex algorithms. I have chosen to use for the DOPA process a simple statistical method to accomplish feature selection in which each metric value is compared to the computed normal value. Although simple, it is effective in identifying abnormal metrics, easy to implement, and able to produce reliable results when used in the DOPA process.

I call the feature selection method I use for identifying metrics outside of normal range "flagging." As noted in Chapter 4, I begin by collecting data from the previous week in order to establish normal ranges for all the metrics during a nonproblematic interval. After establishing the normal values, my code compares each metric at every time instance to the computed normal values that have been established. The program assigns a 0 to every metric that is within the normal range, and it assigns a 1 to every metric that is outside the normal range. This process creates a bitmap of the data set. The metrics outside of normal and identified with a 1 are "flagged" in this way by my process. When a report is generated, only the metrics "flagged" with a 1 are reported and the normal metrics are eliminated. The flagging just described is a very basic method of feature selection.

As I've stated, the statistical method for feature selection used in the DOPA process yields a bitmap of the data set of metric values. The purpose of the flagging process is to reduce the number of data points considered, so in reporting the outcome, we choose to ignore all the metrics with a 0 and report only the metrics flagged with a value of 1. This is what I did initially when I was developing this method. Table 5-1 shows an example of what results look like for a particular problem reported this way. The program sorts the metrics by time and reports only the metrics that are flagged with a 1 (you will see a 1 in FLAG column). The metrics that are furthest from their normal range are reported first for each time interval. The table shown is only a portion of the total results table (what you are viewing is a portion of the metrics from the first time interval). Note: When no feature selection is applied, you would simply see all the metrics, normal (flag value 0) and abnormal (flag value 1), for the time period.

*Table 5-1.* Output example when feature selection is applied; Note: FLAG column value is 1

| STAT_SOURCE | BEGIN_TIME | METRIC_NAME | Value | LOWER_BOUND | UPPER_BOUND | FLAG | AVG All | Variance | StdDev |
|---|---|---|---|---|---|---|---|---|---|
| dba_hist_iostat_function | 2018-05-11 00:00 | Direct Reads small_write_reqs | 33318 | 194 | 20157 | 1 | 3910 | 65994880.5 | 8123.7 |
| dba_hist_iostat_function | 2018-05-11 00:00 | Direct Reads small_write_megabytes | 1939 | 2 | 1341 | 1 | 147 | 356129.1 | 596.8 |
| dba_hist_iostat_function | 2018-05-11 00:00 | Direct Reads small_read_megabytes | 7590 | 302 | 6553 | 1 | 2407 | 4296436.9 | 2072.8 |
| dba_hist_iostat_function | 2018-05-11 00:00 | Direct Reads large_read_megabytes | 1214744 | 52673 | 1137149 | 1 | 477447 | 108801653648.2 | 329851 |
| dba_hist_iostat_function | 2018-05-11 00:00 | Direct Reads large_read_reqs | 1229179 | 58347 | 1166546 | 1 | 493637 | 113201598836.9 | 336454.5 |
| dba_hist_latch | 2018-05-11 00:00 | 7: lob segment query latch gets | 12 | 1 | 5 | 1 | 1 | 3.2 | 1.8 |
| dba_hist_latch | 2018-05-11 00:00 | 3: ILM Stats main anchor latch gets | 206646 | 1548 | 126775 | 1 | 20485 | 2824415625 | 53145.2 |
| dba_hist_latch | 2018-05-11 00:00 | 4: ktm global data spin_gets | 13 | 1 | 8 | 1 | 3 | 7.1 | 2.7 |
| dba_hist_latch | 2018-05-11 00:00 | 4: ktm global data misses | 13 | 1 | 8 | 1 | 3 | 6.9 | 2.6 |
| dba_hist_latch | 2018-05-11 00:00 | 3: cache buffer handles gets | 46902 | 140 | 32145 | 1 | 7813 | 148011255.6 | 12166 |
| dba_hist_latch | 2018-05-11 00:00 | 5: enqueue freelist latch immediate_misses | 56 | 1 | 39 | 1 | 10 | 205.7 | 14.3 |
| dba_hist_latch | 2018-05-11 00:00 | 4: enqueue hash chains spin_gets | 121 | 7 | 110 | 1 | 47 | 977.4 | 31.3 |
| dba_hist_latch | 2018-05-11 00:00 | 3: dml lock allocation gets | 177 | 3 | 163 | 1 | 83 | 1591.2 | 39.9 |
| dba_hist_latch | 2018-05-11 00:00 | 4: enqueue hash chains misses | 131 | 7 | 122 | 1 | 53 | 1173.7 | 34.3 |
| dba_hist_latch | 2018-05-11 00:00 | 7: lob segment dispenser latch gets | 117173 | 55 | 111740 | 1 | 14775 | 2350531728.2 | 48482.3 |
| dba_hist_latch | 2018-05-11 00:00 | 1: begin backup scn array gets | 34234 | 33 | 32675 | 1 | 7230 | 1618599872 | 12722.4 |
| dba_hist_sys_time_model | 2018-05-11 00:00 | INACTIVE_MEMORY_BYTES | 12187103232 | 1052672 | 4495563715 | 1 | 716014510 | 3.57313807263008E18 | 18902746602.4 |
| dba_hist_sys_time_model | 2018-05-11 00:00 | DB time | 42820639481 | 2080415720 | 28341880073 | 1 | 12606719865 | 6.384825394208045E19 | 7990510242.9 |
| dba_hist_sysmetric_summary | 2018-05-11 00:00 | repeated bind elapsed time | 15828139 | 37623 | 12405243 | 1 | 2939045 | 22402224958816.1 | 4733098.9 |
| dba_hist_sysmetric_summary | 2018-05-11 00:00 | Physical Writes Direct Lobs Per Sec | 82 | 1 | 47 | 1 | 16 | 247.5 | 15.7 |
| dba_hist_sysmetric_summary | 2018-05-11 00:00 | Recursive Calls Per Sec | 587 | 14 | 410 | 1 | 212 | 9796.8 | 99 |
| dba_hist_sysmetric_summary | 2018-05-11 00:00 | Total Index Scans Per Sec | 771 | 85 | 698 | 1 | 251 | 50049.9 | 223.7 |
| dba_hist_sysmetric_summary | 2018-05-11 00:00 | Physical Reads Per Sec | 46303 | 2626 | 43679 | 1 | 18941 | 1529885744 | 12368.9 |
| dba_hist_sysmetric_summary | 2018-05-11 00:00 | Physical Read Bytes Per Sec | 379312771 | 21512458 | 357818918 | 1 | 155168038 | 1.026844795143436E16 | 1013125440 |
| dba_hist_sysmetric_summary | 2018-05-11 00:00 | Physical Read Total Bytes Per Sec | 380600426 | 23643609 | 362956259 | 1 | 158135568 | 1.048787891511125E16 | 1024103345.7 |
| dba_hist_sysmetric_summary | 2018-05-11 00:00 | Physical Reads Direct Per Sec | 44049 | 1918 | 42318 | 1 | 18105 | 1465705502.8 | 12106.6 |
| dba_hist_sysmetric_summary | 2018-05-11 00:00 | I/O Megabytes per Second | 366 | 27 | 356 | 1 | 156 | 10006.7 | 100 |
| dba_hist_sysmetric_summary | 2018-05-11 00:00 | Cell Physical IO Interconnect Bytes | 2303332813 | 1680726441 | 2242283135 | 1 | 9838789222 | 3.958670893995504E19 | 6291796956.4 |
| dba_hist_sysstat | 2018-05-11 00:00 | segment prealloc bytes | 2294611968 | 65536 | 660330829 | 1 | 105178515 | 7.7048522864379797E16 | 2775761566.9 |
| dba_hist_sysstat | 2018-05-11 00:00 | securefile bytes non-transformed | 1940433977 | 274532 | 554277935 | 1 | 102184024 | 5.1097226023167381E16 | 2260469554.2 |
| dba_hist_sysstat | 2018-05-11 00:00 | segment dispenser load tasks | 274 | 1 | 83 | 1 | 15 | 1169.6 | 34.2 |

In addition to the actual value of the metric for that time interval (value), you will also see in Table 5-1 the statistical results for AVG All (the mean of all values for that metric), the Variance and StdDev, and the LOWER_BOUND and UPPER_BOUND of normal range for each metric. What I want to draw to your attention at this time is the column FLAG which shows that all of these metrics have a value of 1 in that column.

The flagging process and removal of "normal" values from the data set have reduced the number of data points in the results immensely. While the initial data set of all metrics contained approximately two million rows of data points, the flagged results data set has just a few hundred. As in the clinical blood chemistry generic feature selection example given at the beginning of this chapter, a domain expert is still needed to interpret the results. In the case of Oracle performance analysis, the DBA/tuner is the domain expert and needs to interpret the results. In this example, I've discussed feature selection in the absence of a specific problem case, but in Chapter 8 on case studies, you can see feature selection being applied in the context of real production performance problems.

I found this type of results report (as in Table 5-1) very usable for solving problems when the problem was narrowly defined and occurring across a small time interval (one- to three-hour intervals). However, when I attempted to use it for more poorly defined problems that required me to look at longer time intervals, such as a full 24 hours, I was once again challenged to interpret a very large table of numbers. This prompted me to come up with some refinements that made it easier to interpret the results.

I began my refining process by implementing code to aggregate the flags for all the time intervals in the analysis period and to report the metrics in descending order of flag counts—that is, the metric with the most flagged values reported first and the metric with the least flagged intervals reported last. I included a column in my results table to show how many "flagged" values were identified during the analysis period for that metric. Because I was now dealing with an aggregated set of numbers,

I calculated and included a column to display the average of all the flagged values and the average for all values within that analysis period. When these extra steps were implemented, the results table yielded a more functional tool.

Table 5-2 shows the results for flagging using the enhanced code just described. In this table, each metric is listed only once for the entire analysis period (instead of once for each time interval). The result table is for the same data as that shown in Table 5-1, but in this new format, *Active Parallel Sessions* is listed at the top of the table because it had the greatest number of flagged values in the analysis interval which was a 24-hour period (25 time intervals). FLAG_COUNT shows that there were 16 values outside of normal range for that metric. The average of all 25 intervals (AVG All) was 0, and the average of the 16 metrics that were flagged (AVG Flagged Values) was 4.

*Table 5-2. Results When Flagged Values Are Treated as an Aggregate*

| STAT_SOURCE | METRIC_NAME | FLAG_COUNT | INTERVALS | AVG Flagged Values | LOWER_BOUND | UPPER_BOUND | AVG All |
|---|---|---|---|---|---|---|---|
| dba_hist_sysmetric_summary | Active Parallel Sessions | 16 | 25 | 4 | 0 | 2 | 0 |
| dba_hist_sysmetric_summary | PQ Slave Session Count | 16 | 25 | 4 | 0 | 2 | 0 |
| dba_hist_system_event | Idle: PX Deq: Execute Reply time_waited_micro | 15 | 25 | 3614159291 | 0 | 2321233478 | 316376836 |
| dba_hist_system_event | Idle: PX Deq: Execute Reply time_waited_micro_fg | 15 | 25 | 3614159291 | 0 | 2321233478 | 316376836 |
| dba_hist_sysstat | cleanouts only - consistent read gets | 8 | 25 | 569772 | 316 | 346426 | 79914 |
| dba_hist_sysstat | commit txn count during cleanout | 8 | 25 | 711804 | 2325 | 434219 | 103508 |
| dba_hist_sysstat | sql area purged | 8 | 25 | 711 | 6 | 562 | 187 |
| dba_hist_latch | 1: hash table Sql Plan Finding latch gets | 7 | 25 | 5519 | 357 | 2629 | 771 |
| dba_hist_sys_time_model | failed parse elapsed time | 7 | 25 | 1536484079 | 0 | 761985783 | 86773147 |
| dba_hist_latch | 1: hash table modification latch gets | 7 | 25 | 624 | 16 | 396 | 206 |
| dba_hist_sysstat | parse count (failures) | 7 | 25 | 491 | 0 | 293 | 50 |
| dba_hist_sysstat | sorts (rows) | 7 | 25 | 64908622 | 5894416 | 51916315 | 21792314 |
| dba_hist_iostat_function | Others wait_time | 7 | 25 | 35021780 | 64548 | 30941840 | 10673791 |
| dba_hist_sysstat | parse time elapsed | 6 | 25 | 190281 | 2801 | 105545 | 24985 |
| dba_hist_sysstat | Commit SCN cached | 6 | 25 | 141951 | 230 | 76681 | 16710 |
| dba_hist_sys_time_model | hard parse elapsed time | 6 | 25 | 2222347682 | 21698741 | 1493327057 | 411168804 |
| dba_hist_sysstat | parse time cpu | 6 | 25 | 26306 | 1066 | 15725 | 5429 |
| dba_hist_sys_time_model | parse time elapsed | 6 | 25 | 2263319527 | 39070114 | 1559890802 | 448202115 |
| dba_hist_system_event | Application: SQL: "Net break/reset to client time_waited_micro_fg | 6 | 25 | 15340894 | 0 | 10565940 | 2338365 |
| dba_hist_latch | 1: hash table column usage latch gets | 6 | 25 | 1599 | 163 | 1298 | 639 |
| dba_hist_sysstat | hot buffers moved to head of LRU | 6 | 25 | 3316601 | 115709 | 2735095 | 1425402 |
| dba_hist_sysstat | SCN increments due to another database | 5 | 25 | 277791786 | 12458 | 101882341 | 14785727 |
| dba_hist_system_event | Idle: PX Deq: Execute Reply total_waits | 5 | 25 | 70512 | 0 | 25858 | 2921 |
| dba_hist_system_event | Idle: PX Deq: Execute Reply total_waits_fg | 5 | 25 | 70512 | 0 | 25858 | 2921 |
| dba_hist_latch | 4: process queue reference immediate_gets | 5 | 25 | 72522 | 0 | 30621 | 5192 |
| dba_hist_sysstat | PX local messages recv'd | 5 | 25 | 71688 | 0 | 28611 | 4424 |
| dba_hist_sysstat | PX local messages sent | 5 | 25 | 71688 | 0 | 28611 | 4424 |
| dba_hist_latch | 4: process queue reference gets | 5 | 25 | 1174406 | 1 | 592159 | 88364 |
| dba_hist_system_event | Idle: PX Deq Credit: need buffer time_waited_micro | 5 | 25 | 23460588 | 0 | 11798341 | 2439235 |
| dba_hist_system_event | Idle: PX Deq Credit: need buffer time_waited_micro_fg | 5 | 25 | 23460588 | 0 | 11798341 | 2439235 |
| dba_hist_latch | 1: Real-time descriptor latch misses | 5 | 25 | 220 | 0 | 122 | 23 |
| dba_hist_latch | 1: Real-time descriptor latch sleeps | 5 | 25 | 101 | 0 | 50 | 8 |

This results table is a big improvement over the previous results table because it allows a much easier interpretation of the data. Comparing the two tables, you will see that in Table 5-1, Direct Reads are at the top of the list of metrics for the first hour; this observation might lead you to believe that this is where you should begin tuning efforts. However, when you look at Table 5-2 with the aggregated flagged metrics, you will see that Direct Reads doesn't even appear near the top of the table because it was flagged in only a few intervals (fewer than five since this is where the table cuts off for this example). Instead, what stands out from the second table is that *Active Parallel Sessions* and *PQ Slave Session Count* were both flagged in 16 of the 25 time intervals. This observation is more likely to lead you in the direction of productive tuning efforts.

One further refinement I made to improve my ability to easily interpret the results of the flagging process was to create a flag ratio. My purpose was to help me quantify how far "out of whack" a particular value was. The calculation I use compares the amount the value is beyond either the upper or lower bound to the standard deviation. Essentially, I find the delta between the average flagged values and the upper limit of the range and then divide it by the standard deviation.

When reporting the results of running the code, I can arrange the flag ratio in descending order. As in Table 5-3, this will show me clearly the metrics that are most "out of whack" with the highest flag ratios at the top.

*Table 5-3.* Ordering the Model Output by Flag Ratio

| METRIC_NAME | FLAG_COUNT | AVG Flagged Values | LOWER_BOUND | AVG All | UPPER_BOUND | FLAG_RATIO |
|---|---|---|---|---|---|---|
| transaction tables consistent reads - undo records applied | 7 | 1215819 | 724 | 9713 | 29111 | 90.59 |
| Other: change tracking file synchronous read time_waited_micro | 5 | 1425986348 | 212814 | 415812 | 487582 | 14044.49 |
| deferred (CURRENT) block cleanout applications | 5 | 2521255 | 9867 | 20360 | 26783 | 475.47 |
| Other: change tracking file synchronous read total_waits | 4 | 437374 | 50 | 63 | 67 | 68329.22 |
| Network: SQL*Net more data from client total_waits | 4 | 947371 | 1 | 373 | 640 | 5092.69 |
| Configuration: log file switch completion time_waited_micro | 4 | 95529009 | 33763 | 72164 | 115959 | 2306.75 |
| leaf node splits | 4 | 227169 | 143 | 269 | 467 | 1576.51 |
| write clones created in foreground | 4 | 1965 | 1 | 2 | 5 | 979.88 |
| commit cleanout failures: block lost | 4 | 15369 | 4 | 20 | 40 | 837.64 |
| ▲ calls to kcmgas | 4 | 314780 | 19980 | 29155 | 35423 | 60.9 |
| enqueue releases | 4 | 602254 | 142242 | 186758 | 208372 | 17.7 |
| enqueue requests | 4 | 603170 | 142294 | 187185 | 208656 | 17.58 |
| Enqueue Requests Per Sec | 4 | 169 | 38 | 52 | 57 | 16.51 |
| Other: LGWR worker group ordering time_waited_micro | 4 | 22257637 | 325142 | 1732123 | 3477722 | 14.42 |
| redo buffer allocation retries | 3 | 1702 | 1 | 5 | 9 | 423.33 |
| Network: SQL*Net more data from client time_waited_micro | 3 | 84405142 | 9434 | 167038 | 574481 | 306.76 |
| immediate (CURRENT) block cleanout applications | 3 | 1002303 | 930 | 4843 | 8825 | 250.86 |
| DBWR undo block writes | 3 | 908992 | 1115 | 7436 | 13724 | 164.49 |
| bytes received via SQL*Net from client | 3 | 2764274730 | 10645437 | 29394075 | 51837000 | 159.69 |
| undo change vector size | 3 | 9870801801 | 15011144 | 102777577 | 218673988 | 110.64 |

Each time I run the DOPA process, I am essentially creating a predictive model for determining where in the database a problem is occurring. Any change in the metrics used, the time interval chosen, the sensitivity of flagging, etc., will result in a different and unique feature selection. This is why I call my process a dynamic process. It is adaptable and easily accommodates to manipulation of the attributes being considered.

Feature selection is a very potent tool for solving problems involving extremely large data sets.

In a paper titled, "An Introduction to Variable and Feature Selection," the threefold objective of this tool is clearly expounded:

> *The objective of variable selection is three-fold: improving the prediction performance of the predictors, providing faster and more cost-effective predictors, and providing a better understanding of the underlying process that generated the data. (Guyon and Elisseeff in "An Introduction to Variable and Feature Selection" (PDF)* <http://jmlr.csail.mit.edu/papers/volume3/guyon03a/guyon03a.pdf>*)*

The first two goals are clearly achieved with the flagging method of feature selection used in the DOPA process. We've established that the AWR repository has far too many metrics for a person to evaluate them all, so reducing the number of data points is essential for enabling the performance tuning analyst to make a more accurate diagnosis of the performance problem. Using the DOPA process, he/she does not have to sort through every metric but can consider only the important ones; the tuner can decide which ones are important, not by relying on personal experience or bias to select which metrics to focus on, but by using the flagging method, a highly accurate scientific method for predicting the problem source. The feature selection used for creating the predictive model conserves both time and effort.

The third objective mentioned is the goal of gaining a better understanding of the underlying process. I believe I have only begun to realize this objective, and I can see where further application of the DOPA process may yield even greater impact. This is an idea I will revisit in a later chapter.

# Summary

In this chapter, I have shown how I use the normal ranges established with the statistical methods described earlier and then apply a method of feature selection that compares each metric to the established norms, "flagging" those outside of normal to be included in the predictive model. This flagging draws out the metrics most useful for directing tuning efforts, creating what is referred to as a predictive model.

The predictive model developed by the DOPA process thus far has a high degree of accuracy for finding the root cause of a problem. I refer to the DOPA process as dynamic because it is easily adaptable; each time it is run with slight changes in any number of variables (e.g., time interval, different database, altering the metric sources), it will produce a slightly different predictive model. Feature selection used in this way produces a highly accurate model, but I learned from my son that implementing a taxonomy could augment the usefulness of this analysis even further. Therefore, I have added this additional analytic component; it will be the topic of the next chapter.

When I first started using the feature selection capability of the DOPA process, I had to prove it to myself that it could be useful. After using it for some time in the actual heat of battle, solving performance problems, I am convinced that the DOPA process adds value in many scenarios, especially in scenarios where traditional methods have failed to solve the problem. In Chapter 8 many actual case studies are detailed. Further, the SQL code provided with this book can be used to immediately start building models and seeing results in your own Oracle databases. But before we get to case studies, I want to cover taxonomies (Chapter 6) and some general guidelines on building the models and reporting (Chapter 7).

# CHAPTER 6

# Taxonomy

Feature selection, which was discussed in the last chapter, is a powerful component of the DOPA process. It enables the tuning analyst to quickly identify areas of the database that are performing outside of normal. The metrics with a high incidence of flagged values are assumed to have a high predictive value of pointing to the problem area. And this is definitely true in my experience. While the feature selection/flagging process is sufficient by itself to solve many problems, I learned another analytics "trick" from my son that enabled me to take my analysis one step further. The concept I brought into the analysis is that of taxonomy.

Taxonomy is the process of aggregating/bundling metrics according to some commonality. This is a concept that is used in every field of study. For example, in biology all living things are grouped into six kingdoms (Plantae, Animalia, Fungi, Protista, Eubacteria (Monera), Archaebacteria), and within these larger groupings are subgroups, with even further subgrouping until you get to the level of genus and species.

Taxonomies are used to help structure information. A taxonomic grouping can be organized in a variety of ways. For example, items can be grouped according to physical characteristics, or they can be grouped according to their use. The possibilities for taxonomic groupings are plentiful, but in order to create a useful taxonomy, the MECE principle must be followed. MECE is an acronym for mutually exclusive (ME) and collectively exhaustive (CE). Mutually exclusive (ME) means that every object must map to only one taxonomic group, and collectively exhaustive (CE) refers to the necessity that

© Roger Cornejo 2018
R. Cornejo, *Dynamic Oracle Performance Analytics*,
https://doi.org/10.1007/978-1-4842-4137-0_6

there be a taxonomic group for every item. The easy way to remember this concept is "no gaps (CE) and no overlaps (ME)."

# Why Use Taxonomies?

As stated, the reason for using taxonomy is to help structure information. While flagging metrics allows us to see which metrics are abnormal, the results are still a collection of seemingly unconnected metrics. By creating a taxonomy whereby metrics are grouped according to some commonality, I am essentially bundling the tens of thousands of metrics into a smaller handful of useful higher-level categories to make the analysis easier and more efficient. Doing this allows me to record and see the metric analysis in a new way.

The taxonomy you choose to impose on the metrics will have an intended purpose. With that purpose in mind, you will create categories remembering the MECE principle mentioned above. Following is a discussion of the two taxonomies I have created thus far. Creating a taxonomy for thousands of metrics is no easy task, so I consider the taxonomies I use as a work in progress, whereby I continued to refine them from time to time.

# Infrastructure Taxonomy

The first taxonomic grouping I implemented was an infrastructure taxonomy. The categories I include in this taxonomy are CPU, IO, memory, SQL, DB, and network. Each of these categories also has a subcategory, some of which can be viewed in Figure 6-1. The subcategories for the infrastructure taxonomy were invented by me to provide an extra level of detail to the structure imposed by the taxonomy. The subcategories I assigned stem from personal observations of patterns in the metric names, nothing more. In one sense, the taxonomy is an arbitrary categorization; one could just as easy have another categorization scheme. In Figure 6-1, the metric count column shows how many of the implemented metrics fall into this category/subcategory.

| TAXONOMY_TYPE | CATEGORY | SUB_CATEGORY | METRIC_COUNT |
|---|---|---|---|
| Infrastructure | cpu | concurrency | 11 |
| Infrastructure | cpu | execute | 2 |
| Infrastructure | cpu | limit | 1 |
| Infrastructure | cpu | parallel | 1 |
| Infrastructure | cpu | parse | 8 |
| Infrastructure | cpu | read | 16 |
| Infrastructure | cpu | recursive | 1 |
| Infrastructure | cpu | wait | 1450 |
| Infrastructure | cpu | write | 15 |
| Infrastructure | io | any | 446 |
| Infrastructure | io | concurrency | 5 |
| Infrastructure | io | index | 7 |
| Infrastructure | io | limit | 1 |
| Infrastructure | io | parse | 1 |
| Infrastructure | io | read | 209 |
| Infrastructure | io | recovery | 21 |
| Infrastructure | io | recursive | 1 |
| Infrastructure | io | temp | 57 |
| Infrastructure | io | wait | 218 |
| Infrastructure | io | write | 193 |
| Infrastructure | memory | any | 1484 |
| Infrastructure | memory | concurrency | 27 |
| Infrastructure | memory | limit | 1 |
| Infrastructure | memory | parallel | 12 |
| Infrastructure | memory | read | 26 |
| Infrastructure | memory | recovery | 10 |
| Infrastructure | memory | sessions | 1 |

*Figure 6-1.* *This table shows a portion of the infrastructure taxonomy with its categories and subcategories*

The goal of the infrastructure taxonomy is to group metrics into functional groups that will help identify when a performance issue is related to a problem in the infrastructure and direct to the specific portion of the infrastructure. What I have done is match metrics to the area within the technology infrastructure [sometimes referred to the technology stack] that best fits the metric.

When a taxonomy is used within the DOPA process, the interpretation of the results is made much easier. For example, when lots of metrics are flagged and the taxonomy shows that they are all related to the *memory* category, it is obviously prudent to consider that changes to memory might be an important part of the solution. Likewise, if a lot of metrics flag up in the *CPU* or *IO* categories, one would need to check into these infrastructure components to see if they are operating efficiently. By reporting metrics along with the taxonomic grouping, these observations are more easily interpreted.

When you run the DOPA process using the infrastructure taxonomy, you will get a table that shows the taxonomic categories (or subcategories if you choose to look at this level) and the category count. The *category count view* shows how many metrics were flagged in that category for the time interval specified. Figure 6-2 shows the results of the DOPA process looking at the category count view using the infrastructure taxonomy for a real data set. In this example, you can see that the *IO* category has a significant number of flagged metrics. There are other areas with flagged metrics, but because of the overwhelming number of flagged metrics in the *IO* category, a closer look at those would be a good next step.

| TAXONOMY_TYPE | CATEGORY | CATEGORY_COUNT |
|---|---|---|
| Infrastructure | io | 162 |
| Infrastructure | cpu | 70 |
| Infrastructure | sql | 66 |
| Infrastructure | memory | 33 |
| Infrastructure | any | 13 |
| Infrastructure | network | 7 |
| Infrastructure | db | 7 |

*Figure 6-2.* *This table shows the results of the DOPA process looking at the category count view using the infrastructure taxonomy for a real data set.*

In order to build the infrastructure taxonomy, I wrote a single SQL statement that examines every single metric instrumented thus far. The SQL code searches for specific keywords in the metric name and uses them to classify the metric into one of the categories and subcategories. The search includes terms like i/o, memory, and network. If I can't classify a metric into a high-level category, I give it the classification "any" [metrics in the *any* category, of course, are good candidates for refining the taxonomy when the time comes]. After running this search/ categorization, I check to make sure assigned categories make sense. I use an iterative process to refine the substrings so that I can be sure each metric gets to a proper categorization. As I said, my taxonomy is a work in progress; I continue to make modifications as I see the need to change things around.

# Oracle Taxonomy

The second taxonomy I created classifies according to Oracle subcomponents/subsystems. Since Oracle is a massive system with many working parts, and since many of those parts are managed independently, it is helpful to know if performance issues are affecting one or more of those parts so that we may focus our tuning efforts there. Figure 6-3 shows some of the classification groups I use for this taxonomy. You can see in this figure that the categories have subcategories as well. In the table, the first category you will see is *BUFFER CACHE*. *BUFFER CACHE* is further divided into two subcategories: ratio and time. There is one metric in each of these subcategories as indicated in the metric count column.

| TAXONOMY_TYPE | CATEGORY | SUB_CATEGORY | METRIC_COUNT |
|---|---|---|---|
| Oracle | BUFFER CACHE | RATIO | 1 |
| Oracle | BUFFER CACHE | TIME | 1 |
| Oracle | COMPRESSION | ALL | 15 |
| Oracle | COMPRESSION | COUNT | 1 |
| Oracle | CONNECTION | TIME | 1 |
| Oracle | DATA PUMP | ALL | 9 |
| Oracle | DATA PUMP | TIME | 1 |
| Oracle | DBWR | ALL | 19 |
| Oracle | DBWR | TIME | 1 |
| Oracle | DBWR | WORKLOAD | 2 |
| Oracle | DIRECT I/O | ALL | 18 |
| Oracle | DIRECT I/O | TIME | 2 |
| Oracle | EXTERNAL TABLE | ALL | 6 |
| Oracle | EXTERNAL TABLE | TIME | 12 |
| Oracle | IN-MEMORY | ALL | 9 |
| Oracle | IN-MEMORY | TIME | 1 |
| Oracle | JAVA | ALL | 12 |
| Oracle | JAVA | COUNT | 12 |
| Oracle | JAVA | TIME | 1 |
| Oracle | LGWR | ALL | 19 |
| Oracle | LGWR | TIME | 21 |
| Oracle | LOCKING | ALL | 7337 |

***Figure 6-3.*** *This table shows some of the categories used for taxonomy organized around Oracle's subcomponents/subsystems*

To create the Oracle taxonomy, I use the same SQL code I used for creating the infrastructure taxonomy, but I use different keywords that relate to the Oracle subcomponents to search and assign each metric to the appropriate category. To be clear, the categories and subcategories were created by using patterns in the metric names for the assignments.

I ran the DOPA code using the Oracle taxonomy on the same data that was used for the infrastructure taxonomy example in Figure 6-2, and those results are shown in Figure 6-4. When running the category count view using the Oracle taxonomy, many of flagged metrics currently fall into the *ALL* category. This is because I have not spent a great deal of time assigning metrics to the various categories. I include this to show that the taxonomies are only as useful as you make them. I intend to go back and improve this particular taxonomy as time allows because I think there is good potential for its usefulness when it is fleshed out a little better.

| TAXONOMY_TYPE | CATEGORY | CATEGORY_COUNT |
|---|---|---|
| Oracle | ALL | 259 |
| Oracle | REDO | 25 |
| Oracle | DIRECT I/O | 16 |
| Oracle | PARSE | 7 |
| Oracle | OS STAT | 7 |
| Oracle | UNDO | 7 |
| Oracle | STREAMS | 6 |
| Oracle | LGWR | 5 |
| Oracle | LOCKING | 5 |
| Oracle | BUFFER CACHE | 5 |
| Oracle | OTHERS | 4 |
| Oracle | COMPRESSION | 3 |
| Oracle | BACKGROUND | 3 |
| Oracle | RESMGR | 3 |
| Oracle | DBWR | 3 |

***Figure 6-4.*** *This table shows the results of the DOPA process looking at the category count view using the Oracle taxonomy for the same data set used in the infrastructure taxonomy in Figure 6-2*

# The Taxonomy Table

I created a single Oracle table to persist the taxonomic classification of the metrics for both taxonomies [actually, any number of taxonomies can be persisted in this table]. The actual SQL code I used is several hundred lines long and can be found in:

AWR - flag - all metrics - taxonomy.sql

The code contains the SQL used to create the taxonomy table and populate it with data for the infrastructure and Oracle taxonomies. The result of running this SQL statement is a populated table called METRIC_TAXONOMY.

A portion of the data dictionary view of the taxonomy table is shown in Figure 6-5. The taxonomy table has five rows.

**TAXONOMY_TYPE** is the name for the taxonomy. Currently I have implemented infrastructure and Oracle taxonomy types.

**STAT_SOURCE** displays the name of the view that provides the data for a given metric source of the metric.

**METRIC_NAME** is the name for that metric as given or as built during the normalization process.

**CATEGORY** and **SUB_CATEGORY** specify the taxonomic groupings.

| ID | Column Name | Data Type | Num Distinct |
|----|-------------|-----------|--------------|
| 1 | TAXONOMY_TYPE | VARCHAR2 (14 Byte) | 2 |
| 2 | STAT_SOURCE | VARCHAR2 (26 Byte) | 7 |
| 3 | METRIC_NAME | VARCHAR2 (151 Byte) | 11138 |
| 4 | CATEGORY | VARCHAR2 (14 Byte) | 36 |
| 5 | SUB_CATEGORY | VARCHAR2 (11 Byte) | 21 |

***Figure 6-5.*** *This is a description of the taxonomy table from the Oracle dictionary view, USER_TAB_COLUMNS*

A portion of the taxonomy table is shown in Figure 6-6. In this sample listing of the metric taxonomy table, both taxonomy types are included. The table displays the category and subcategory into which each metric has been sorted. The source(s) of each metric is also given. I believe it is important to carry the metric source, because I don't want users of the DOPA process to lose sight of the source from which each metric value came. An interesting observation here is that *DB time* is a metric with values drawn from two different sources.

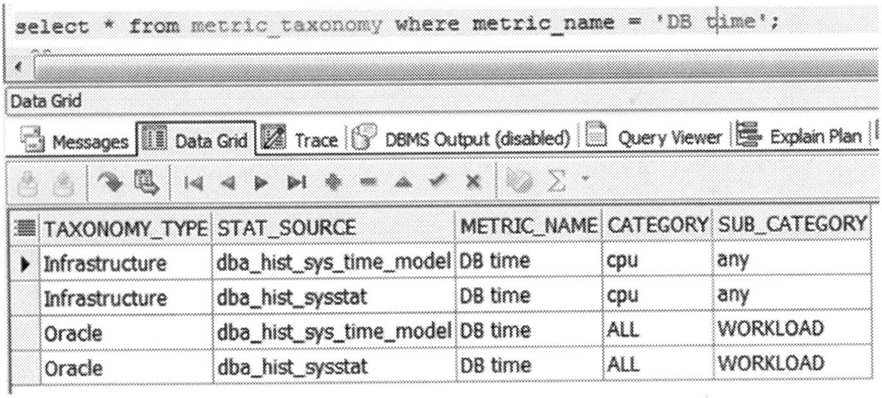


| TAXONOMY_TYPE | STAT_SOURCE | METRIC_NAME | CATEGORY | SUB_CATEGORY |
|---|---|---|---|---|
| Infrastructure | dba_hist_sys_time_model | DB time | cpu | any |
| Infrastructure | dba_hist_sysstat | DB time | cpu | any |
| Oracle | dba_hist_sys_time_model | DB time | ALL | WORKLOAD |
| Oracle | dba_hist_sysstat | DB time | ALL | WORKLOAD |

***Figure 6-6.*** *This figure shows a portion of the taxonomy table. It displays the taxonomy types with the category and subcategory into which each metric has been classified along with the source(s) of each metric.*

Having a single table for both (or more) taxonomies allows you to use it in the DOPA process based on the taxonomic classification that makes the most sense for your use case (i.e., the model you are building). It also allows you to subset the model in multiple ways which can be helpful for discovering patterns and identifying particular areas of performance degradation. As I build models using the DOPA process, I have always picked one or the other of the two taxonomies.

Again, both of the taxonomies I have developed thus far are a work in progress. I am always striving to adhere to the MECE principle and want to have good/useful categorizations for the metrics. If I notice that an important metric is categorized inappropriately, I adjust the code that builds the taxonomy. I simply drop the old taxonomy table and create a new one with the new mappings of the metrics to the taxonomic categories. My infrastructure taxonomy has been the more helpful to me thus far, but that is probably because it comports well with the DOPA process model building I have been using most.

# Code Snippet for Building the Taxonomies

As stated above, I use the same SQL code to create both the infrastructure and the Oracle taxonomies. I use the CTAS (create table as select) method where the select statement is pulling the metric names and sources from a "view"/subquery that represents the total set of instrumented normalized metrics [the collection of metrics and normalization was covered in Chapter 3—Data Preparation]. I have two select statements (one for the infrastructure taxonomy and one for the Oracle taxonomy) unioned together. In the select lists, I use case statements and different keywords to assign each metric to the appropriate category and subcategory. A code snippet from "AWR - flag - all metrics - taxonomy.sql" is provided in the following.

```
select 'Infrastructure' taxonomy_type
, stat_source, metric_name
, case when stat_source = 'dba_hist_iostat_function' then 'io'
       when upper(metric_name) like '% IO %' then 'io'
       when upper(metric_name) like '%BUFFER BUSY%' then 'io'
       -- ...
       when upper(metric_name) like '%CURSOR' then 'memory'
       when upper(metric_name) like '%CACHE%' then 'memory'
       -- ...
```

```
        when upper(metric_name) like '%REDO%' then 'sql'
        when upper(metric_name) like 'APPLICATION:%' then 'sql'

        when upper(metric_name) like 'DB TIME' then 'cpu'
        when upper(metric_name) like '%CPU%' then 'cpu'
        -- ...
        when upper(metric_name) like '%SQL*NET%' then 'network'
        when upper(metric_name) like '%NETWORK%' then 'network'
        -- ...
        when upper(metric_name) like '%LIMIT%' then 'db'
        when upper(metric_name) like '%ROLLBACKS%' then 'db'
        -- ...
        else 'any'
    end as category
, case when stat_source = 'dba_hist_system_event' then 'wait'
        when upper(metric_name) like '%WAIT%' then 'wait'
        -- ...
        when upper(metric_name) like '%READ%' then 'read'
        -- ...
        when upper(metric_name) like '%WRITE%' then 'write'
        when upper(metric_name) like '%CHECKPOINT%' then 'write'
        -- ...
        when upper(metric_name) like '%PARSE%' then 'parse'
        -- ...
        when upper(metric_name) like '%CURSORS%' then 'cursors'
        -- ...
        when upper(metric_name) like '%REDO%' then 'recovery'
        when upper(metric_name) like '%UNDO%' then 'recovery'
        -- ...
        when upper(metric_name) like '%PARALLEL%' then 'parallel'
```

```
        when upper(metric_name) like '%PX%' then 'parallel'
        -- ...
        when upper(metric_name) like '%ENQUEUE%' then
        'concurrency'
        when upper(metric_name) like '%CONCURRENCY%' then
        'concurrency'
        -- ...
        else 'any'
    end as sub_category
from (select distinct stat_source, metric_name from metrics )
        /* "metrics" is the set of all normalized metrics */
-- ...
union ALL
-- ...

select 'Oracle' taxonomy_type
, stat_source, metric_name
, case
        when stat_source = 'dba_hist_latch' then 'LOCKING'
        when stat_source = 'dba_hist_osstat' then 'OS STAT'
        when upper(metric_name) like '%ENQUEUE%' then 'LOCKING'
        when upper(metric_name) like 'REDO%'  then 'REDO'
        when upper(metric_name) like '%LOG WRITE%'  then 'REDO'
        when upper(metric_name) like '%: LOG %'  then 'REDO'
        when upper(metric_name) like 'ARCH%'  then 'ARCH'
        when upper(metric_name) like '%PGA%'  then 'PGA'
        when upper(metric_name) like '%SGA%'  then 'SGA'
        when upper(metric_name) like '%UNDO%' then 'UNDO'
        when upper(metric_name) like '%DBWR%' then 'DBWR'
        when upper(metric_name) like '%LGWR%' then 'LGWR'
        when upper(metric_name) like '%RMAN%' then 'RMAN'
        when upper(metric_name) like '%RESMGR%' then 'RESMGR'
```

```
        -- ...
        when upper(metric_name) like '%DATA PUMP%' then 'DATA PUMP'
        when upper(metric_name) like 'DIRECT %E%S%' then 'DIRECT I/O'
        when upper(metric_name) like '%HEATMAP%' then 'COMPRESSION'
        else 'ALL'
    end as category
, case when upper(metric_name) like 'DB CPU' then 'WORKLOAD'
        when upper(metric_name) like 'ROWS PER SORT' then 'WORKLOAD'
        when upper(metric_name) like '%LOAD%' then 'WORKLOAD'
        -- ...
        when upper(metric_name) like '%PER TXN%' then 'WORKLOAD'
        when upper(metric_name) like 'DB TIME' then 'WORKLOAD'
        when upper(metric_name) like '%TIME%' then 'TIME'
        when upper(metric_name) like '%LATENCY%' then 'LATENCY'
        when upper(metric_name) like '%RATIO%' then 'RATIO'
        when upper(metric_name) like '%COUNT%' then 'COUNT'
        else 'ALL'
    end as sub_category
from (select distinct stat_source, metric_name from metrics  )
        /* "metrics" is the set of all normalized metrics */
order by 3,1,2
;
```

This hard-coded approach to building the taxonomies works, but it is a bit cumbersome, but it works well enough for my purposes. In the future, I hope to explore the possibility of using machine learning techniques to build additional taxonomies.

# Summary

The main purpose of this chapter was to introduce you to the concept of taxonomies. Building a taxonomy means simply creating meaningful categories into which the various metrics can be sorted/organized. The selection of which category scheme to use will be determined by your own needs/interests. For example, you could create a taxonomy to map a metric to where it can be found in the AWR report if that was important to you. Similarly, one could develop a taxonomy that maps a metric to where it appears in Oracle Enterprise Manager. Any categorization scheme is possible as long as you adhere to the MECE principle—mutually exclusive and collectively exhaustive. The instructions provided in this chapter, along with the SQL code in "AWR - flag - all metrics - taxonomy.sql," will equip you to enhance the current taxonomies or build your own custom taxonomies to enhance your understanding of previously selected features using string pattern matching.

Another purpose of this chapter was to show you how a simple technique can be a powerful means to improve the DOPA process. The usefulness of taxonomic groupings lies to a great extent in the reporting phase of the DOPA process, and that is the topic of the next chapter where you will learn how to use the taxonomies to bring a greater depth of insight to tuning analytics.

# CHAPTER 7

# Building the Model and Reporting

In the preceding chapters, I introduced the individual steps of the DOPA process. It is finally time to put it all together, build the model, and report the results. As I have repeated throughout the book, the DOPA process is dynamic. You essentially create a new, unique predictive model with each execution of the code by altering the model inputs as you refine your tuning efforts. It is also versatile because the data can be subset in such a way that it makes the analysis easy and clearly shows the metrics that enable you to discover the cause of the performance problem.

In this chapter, I'll discuss the model-building process including the selection of variables used as input and how to make those choices and the output views.

## Bringing Together the DOPA Process Components

In prior chapters, we detailed each of the steps/components of the DOPA process:

- Selecting the metrics data sources

- Normalizing the data: unpivoting to form key-value pair structure

© Roger Cornejo 2018
R. Cornejo, *Dynamic Oracle Performance Analytics*,
https://doi.org/10.1007/978-1-4842-4137-0_7

- Removing outliers for normal range calculations

- Establishing normal ranges for metric values

- Integrating metrics with taxonomies

- Flagging metrics that are outside of the normal ranges

The DOPA process I've developed uses a single SQL statement to accomplish these steps with the result being a distillation of the set of all metrics within the retention period down to only the metrics with unusual values (mostly high values) for a given problem interval. This chapter will detail the various methods used for this distillation which is essentially a process of subsetting the data. Before discussing the methods however, I want to explain in more detail the subsetting itself.

Figure 7-1 provides a graphical representation of the subsetting that occurs as part of the DOPA process.

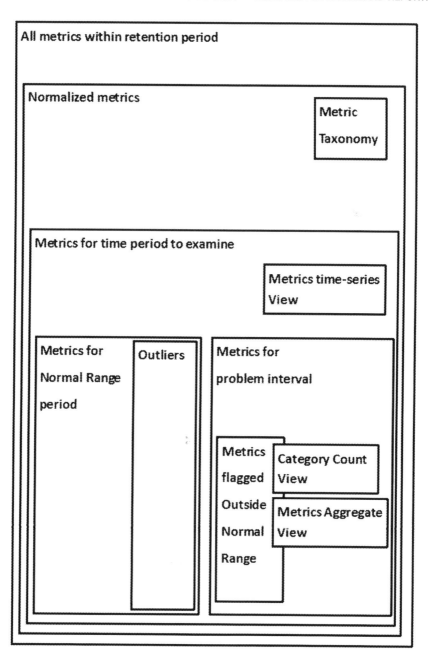

***Figure 7-1.*** *A graphical representation of the subset refinement within the DOPA process*

The large outer box represents the set of all metrics available within the retention period. Since I'm currently only instrumenting AWR metrics, it is more specifically the set of all AWR metrics within the retention period.

From that all-encompassing starting point, a subset of metrics are normalized and included in the DOPA process. (The details of this data preparation step are covered in Chapter 3—Data Preparation. The taxonomies are built from the normalized metrics as well and are covered in detail in Chapter 6—Taxonomy.)

When I am ready to build a model and report, I further subset the normalized metrics as follows.

First, I subset on the number of days back. The reason for subsetting the normalized metrics by the number of days back is that in some cases there is a month or more of AWR metrics and I usually don't need to look at all of them.

A further subsetting involves choosing a date range from which to calculate the normal ranges; this is a smaller subset that focuses in on a period that is "nonproblematic." (The details regarding normal ranges and outlier removal are in Chapter 4—Statistical Analysis, and the thought process that guides your selection of a normal range data set is covered in a subsequent section of this chapter [see section "Variables for Building the Model"].) Outliers excluded from the normal calculation are shown as a smaller box inside this set.

The problem interval represents the other subsets of the chosen date range. The DOPA process analysis relies on a comparison of the problem interval to the norms established using the "nonproblematic" interval. Metrics found to be outside of normal range based on this comparison will be "flagged" and are represented as a smaller subset within this interval. The metric taxonomy is merged into the analysis by this point as well.

When reporting the results of the model, I choose to view the flagged metrics using one of two views, either the Category Count View which yields a high-level picture or the Metrics Aggregate View for a metric by metric detailed view of the model.

For drill-down analysis purposes, I may also use a third view, the Metrics Time-Series View (usually for a single metric), to see how a particular metric has behaved over time. This view will allow me to see all the data for a particular metric, not only the flagged values, for a specified time range. I often graph this in Excel so that I can visually see the metric trend over time.

The three views are detailed in subsequent sections of this chapter.

Some minds may better understand the DOPA process as a data flow, so I developed Figure 7-2 to depict the DOPA process as a data flow.

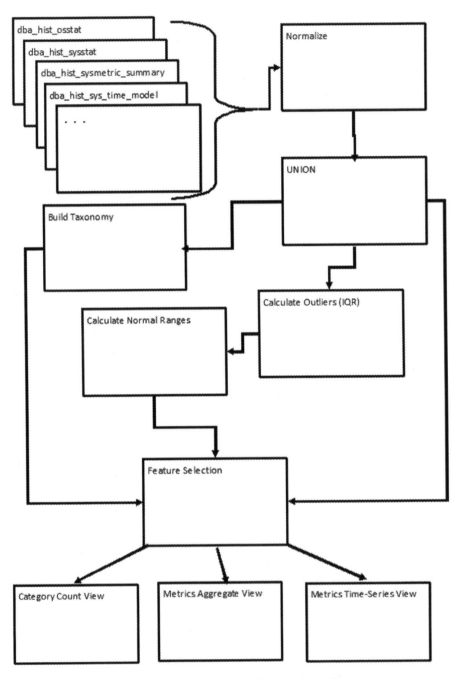

***Figure 7-2.*** *The DOPA process depicted as a data flow*

The data flow figure can be understood as follows:

- Metrics are normalized from the set of metrics to be instrumented.

- These normalized metrics are unioned together for analysis.

- The taxonomies are built from the normalized metrics prior to running the DOPA process.

- From the unionized normalized metrics, outliers are computed and normal ranges calculated.

- The main DOPA feature selection process builds the model by merging in the unioned metrics, the normal ranges, and the taxonomy, then does some basic flagging, and exposes the results of the model in one of the three views: Category Count View, Metrics Aggregate View, and Metrics Time-Series View.

Now that you have seen an overview of the DOPA process as both a series of refined subsets of metrics and as a data flow, I will discuss the SQL code I developed and then how to actually begin building metrics-based models of specific Oracle performance problems.

# Implementing the DOPA Process: The SQL Code

There are a few relevant SQL statements involved with the DOPA process that I developed. This work is offered as a professional courtesy, "as-is," and without warranty. I disclaim any liability for damages that may result from using this code. I developed this code mostly under Oracle versions 11g and 12c; it will not work in Oracle version 10g since some AWR changes in the more recent versions were not available in 10g. It is a simple task

to make the modifications needed to run this under 10g [DBA_HIST_
IOSTAT_FUNCTION is not in 10g and thus needs to be removed from
instrumentation to run this under 10g]. Further, I use this code from Toad
which understands the substitution variables prefixed with a ":". Since I've
not run this from other environments, I don't know how it will behave
there, although I suspect it will run as-is in, say, SQL Developer or other
similar tools.

# Precondition to Running the DOPA Process

When I encounter a database where I've not yet used the DOPA process, I
first create the taxonomy table and populate it with data using the create
table statement in the file:

>AWR - flag - all metrics - taxonomy.sql

The result of running this SQL statement is a populated table called
METRIC_TAXONOMY.

# Running the DOPA Process

When I'm ready to build a model and run the dynamic analysis, I use one
or more of the following SQL statements based on which view is of interest
at the time. The SQL code in these files is essentially the same except for
the particular "view" they select from [the "view" is actually a named
subquery in the WITH clause part of the SQL statement].

>AWR - flag - all metrics – Category Count View.sql

>AWR - flag - all metrics – Metrics Aggregate View.sql

>AWR - flag - all metrics – Metrics Time-Series View.sql

The output from these views is described in detail in the following
section.

# Documenting Model Parameters

If I care to document the parameters I've used for a particular model, I run
the following SQL statement:

> AWR - flag - all metrics - Model Parameters.sql

Example output from running this SQL:

| PARAM_NAME | PARAM_VALUE | DEFAULT_VALUE | DESCRIPTION |
|---|---|---|---|
| :taxonomy_type | Infrastructure | Infrastructure | to subset on this metric |
| :category | NULL | NULL | optional: to subset on this metric |
| :sub_category | NULL | NULL | optional: to subset on this metric |
| :stats_days_back_only_Y_N | N | N | optional: easy way to set a problem interval date range |
| :stats_days_back | 10 | NULL | optional: specify a number of days back |
| :allint_st_MM_DD_YYYY_HH24_MI | 08_14_2018_20_00 | NULL | Start date/time for all metrics |
| :allint_end_MM_DD_YYYY_HH24_MI | 08_25_2018_10_00 | NULL | End date/time for all metrics |
| :intrvl_st_MM_DD_YYYY_HH24_MI | 08_23_2018_20_00 | NULL | Start date/time for the problem interval |
| :intrvl_end_MM_DD_YYYY_HH24_MI | 08_24_2018_10_00 | NULL | End date/time for the problem interval |
| :normRng_st_MM_DD_YYYY_HH24_MI | 08_15_2018_20_00 | NULL | Start date/time for the normal ranges interval |
| :normRng_end_MM_DD_YYYY_HH24_MI | 08_16_2018_10_00 | NULL | End date/time for the normal ranges interval |
| :dba_hist_sys_time_model | Y | Y | Use "Y" to include this data source in the analysis |
| :metric_name | NULL | NULL | to subset :metric_name like <> |
| :inst_id | NULL | NULL | optional: to specify an instance number as in RAC environments |
| :dba_hist_sysstat | Y | Y | Use "Y" to include this data source in the analysis |
| :dba_hist_osstat | Y | Y | Use "Y" to include this data source in the analysis |
| :dba_hist_iostat_function | Y | Y | Use "Y" to include this data source in the analysis |
| :dba_hist_sysmetric_summary | Y | Y | Use "Y" to include this data source in the analysis |
| :dba_hist_system_event | Y | Y | Use "Y" to include this data source in the analysis |
| :dba_hist_latch | N | N | Use "N" to exclude this data source in the analysis |
| :iqr_factor | 1.5 | 1.5 | to define a different inter-quartile range factor |
| :Q1_PERCENTILE | .25 | .25 | to specify different lower percentile (default is 1st quartile) |
| :Q3_PERCENTILE | .75 | .75 | to specify different upper percentile (default is 3rd quartile) |
| :stat_source | NULL | NULL | to subset on a single STAT_SOURCE |
| :flagged_values_only_Y_N | N | NULL | usually set to Y - exception: "N" for Metric Time-Series |
| :flag_ratio | 0 | 0.00 | to subset on metrics with flag_ratio values > = to specified flag_ratio |

# Variables for Building the Model

As I have emphasized, the DOPA process is a dynamic process. It involves
running the code against a set of persisted time-based metrics and refining
the set of all metrics within the retention period down to the metrics which
have unusual values and are likely to be key influencers impacting the
performance issue.

By altering variables to meet the needs of that run, a unique model is built. Each run of the code builds a unique model and yields a unique output in the form of a view. These views are easily interpreted and useful for predicting the cause of performance issues. By iterating through this model-building process, a tuner is able to gain a good picture of how the database is performing and where performance issues are occurring.

The variables/inputs chosen will determine the output. Therefore, a careful choosing will yield the best results. In the next section, I describe the set of variables I have included in my code. When writing your own code, you may choose to use more or less variables as per your needs. Later in the chapter, I will discuss in greater detail the thought process behind building the model and how and why you might want to alter these variable inputs to maximize the predictive value of the model-building process.

Here is a list of the input parameters that can be modified:

**Date ranges impacting the model**: As described in the DOPA process subsetting in the preceding text, there are three sets of date ranges of interest:

1.  The total time period that you want to examine

2.  The time period during which the problem manifested

3.  The time period from which normal ranges will be calculated

These date ranges are essential to the model-building process as they define the set of time-series metrics which will be included in the various parts of the DOPA process. The following descriptions provide the essential details:

1.  *The total time period that you want to examine* (a.k.a. Date Range of Metric Data to Examine): This will be the beginning and end date/time intervals from which you pull the metric values to examine.

Since Oracle persists AWR metrics for a set retention period (typically 1–4 weeks and even up to 120 days in environments I've worked in) and you may not need to examine all the data in that period, this should be subset to a reasonable number of days. I currently use the number of days back to examine and set this time interval ~one week of historic data. You can just as easily choose to do a few hours or several days' worth of metric collection.

2. *The time period during which the problem manifested* (a.k.a. Date Range for Problem Interval): This will be the beginning and end date/time intervals during which the problem was reported to occur. It will necessarily be within the Date Range of Metric Data to Examine.

3. *The time period from which to calculate the normal ranges* (a.k.a. Date Range for Establishing Normals): This will be the beginning and end date/time intervals that will provide the metric values for establishing the metric normal ranges. This must also be a subset of the larger Date Range of Metric Data to Examine. It usually makes most sense for the Date Range for Establishing Normals to be outside of the Date Range for Problem Interval since we want this to represent a nonproblematic operation of the database.

**Taxonomies of interest**: I have two taxonomies currently implemented (infrastructure and Oracle), so I have put this as a variable so that I can easily use one or the other. If you were to implement other taxonomies, they would be subset here as well. To leverage the most out of the taxonomies, I allow choosing a taxonomy via subsetting on the following taxonomy columns [described fully in Chapter 6—Taxonomy]:

> **Taxonomy type**: the name of the taxonomy
>
> **Category**: the high-level category within that taxonomy
>
> **Subcategory**: the subcategory within the higher-level category

Remember that in order to make use of the taxonomy for a given database, the taxonomy will need to be built prior to the run (refer to Chapter 6 for instructions on how to do this).

> **Metric sources**: This variable allows you to choose the metric sources from which you will pull data. You can choose any or all of the metric sources that have been implemented.
>
> **Metric name**: By setting this as a variable, I can subset on a single metric name or set of metric names using the wildcard character, "%". This is useful for deep-dive analysis once you have narrowed in on the problem area.
>
> **Outlier sensitivity settings**: For identifying outliers, my default is to identify as an outlier any value 1.5 times the interquartile range (IQR) below Q1 and above Q3. I have coded the "IQR factor" as a variable, thus allowing me to tweak the outlier removal sensitivity if/when there is a need to do so.

**Flagged values**: The DOPA process can be used to report all metric values, not just the flagged metric values. To accomplish this in my code, I indicate whether I want to include only the flagged metric values in my report (Y) or all the metric values (N).

**Flag ratio**: This is a calculated number representing how many standard deviations from normal the metric value is (i.e., how far "out of whack" the metric value is). I implemented this as a variable so that I can modify the flag ratio to suit my needs. Using this variable, I can subset data based on the flag ratio I choose. The flag ratio is explained in detail in Chapter 4 on statistics.

# Reporting

Running the code once you have set your variables will produce a predictive model in tabular format. You will choose which "view" to display [I use the term "view" in a generic sense—not meaning an Oracle object know as a view]. The DOPA process output can be presented in one of the following three views:

1. Category Count View

2. Metrics Aggregate View

3. Metrics Time-Series View

Each of the views is described below. Following the description of each view, there is a table which displays a complete list of the column names in that view and a short description of it. You may choose to include more or less columns in the views you develop for this process. Because I'm using Toad to format the output, the columns included in the view can be moved around and/or removed and this is useful for analysis too. It allows me to see more or less information based on the need without having to change the code.

The *Category Count View* displays the results according to taxonomic groupings. This is a helpful way to view the data to gain a bird's-eye view of what is going on in the database and whether there is one or more than one area of trouble. Figure 7-3 describes the columns of this view.

| Report: Metrics Category Count View | | |
|---|---|---|
| Report Column | Description | Example Value |
| TAXONOMY_TYPE | The name of the taxonomy | Infrastructure |
| CATEGORY | The category assigned to the metric | memory |
| CATEGORY_COUNT | the number of times a metric in that category was flagged | 58 |

***Figure 7-3.*** *Column names and descriptions for Report: Metrics Category Count View*

The *Metrics Aggregate View* displays the number of flags for each metric, number of intervals flagged, average flag value, flag ratio, and average all. I use this view to provide an overall picture of what is going on with respect to unusual performance metrics during the problem interval. It is concise and easy to interpret because the metric information has been consolidated—there is only one line in the table for each metric. Figure 7-4 describes the columns of this view.

**Report: Metrics Aggregate View**

| Report Column | Description | Example Value |
|---|---|---|
| TAXONOMY_TYPE | The name of the taxonomy | Infrastructure |
| CATEGORY | The category assigned to the metric | memory |
| SUB_CATEGORY | The sub-category assigned to the metric | sessions |
| STAT_SOURCE | The AWR View from which Metrics are sourced | dba_hist_sysmetric_summary |
| METRIC_NAME | The name of the metric | Session Count |
| FLAG_COUNT | number of times a metric was flagged in a problem interval | 10 |
| INTERVALS | number of snapshots in the problem interval | 24 |
| AVG Flagged Values | The average value of the metric across the problem interval | 1,058 |
| LOWER_BOUND | The lower bound of the normal range | 570 |
| UPPER_BOUND | The upper bound of the normal range | 1,258 |
| FLAG_RATIO | The calculated flag ratio | 1.34 |
| FLAG_EVAL | A visual representation of the flag ratio | ••• |
| FLAG | 0 for inside normal range ; 1 for outside of normal range | 0 or 1 |
| AVG All | The average value of the metric across all intervals examined | 927 |

***Figure 7-4.*** *Column names and descriptions for Report: Metrics Aggregate View*

The *Metrics Time-Series View* displays metric data for each time instance whether or not it was flagged. This view is very useful for deep-dive analysis once a problem area has been identified. It gives the data for every instance during the interval. Figure 7-5 describes the columns of this view.

**Report: Metrics Time-Series View**

| Report Column | Description | Example Value |
|---|---|---|
| TAXONOMY_TYPE | The name of the taxonomy | Infrastructure |
| CATEGORY | The category assigned to the metric | memory |
| SUB_CATEGORY | The sub-category assigned to the metric | sessions |
| STAT_SOURCE | The AWR View from which Metrics are sourced | dba_hist_sysmetric_summary |
| SNAP_ID | The AWR Snap Id the metric was measured in | 48743 |
| BEGIN_TIME | The begin interval time from dba_hist_snapshot | 2018-06-29 08:00 |
| METRIC_NAME | The name of the metric | Session Count |
| AVERAGE | The value of the metric as measured by AWR in that interval | 1,497 |
| LOWER_BOUND | The lower bound of the normal range | 570 |
| UPPER_BOUND | The upper bound of the normal range | 1,258 |
| FLAG_RATIO | The calculated flag ratio | 1.34 |
| FLAG_EVAL | A visual representation of the flag ratio | *** |
| FLAG | 0 for inside normal range ; 1 for outside of normal range | 0 or 1 |
| VARIANCE_AVERAGE | 0 for inside normal range ; 31,827 for outside of normal range | 31,827 |
| STDDEV_AVERAGE | 0 for inside normal range ; 178 for outside of normal range | 178 |
| AVERAGE_VALUE | 0 for inside normal range ; 927 for outside of normal range | 927 |

***Figure 7-5.*** *Column names and descriptions for Report: Metrics Time-Series View*

As I said before, you might decide to add other views of interest, but the abovementioned views are the ones I have coded in the DOPA process for my own use. At the end of this chapter, you will see examples of these views and how they are used for the analysis.

# General Instructions for Building and Tweaking the Model

Since building a model is running the DOPA process for a set of input conditions, I am going to discuss the thought pattern I use for selecting the subset conditions to address various problems. Later in this chapter, I show an example of how the model is used to determine next steps based on the results of the first model. In Chapter 8 on case studies, there are a good number of real problems and how the DOPA process was used to solve them. These case studies provide a more detailed picture of the DOPA process in action.

Upon learning of a performance problem on a particular database, I collect as much relevant information as I can from the user. You can refer back to Chapter 2 on gathering problem information for more specifics on the information I try to obtain. One important thing to consider is that it can be very helpful for the normal range calculations to get a date/time range not only for the problem interval but also for when the performance was normal or acceptable. Having gathered as much relevant information as possible, I set the variables for building the model. The decision-making process for which inputs are selected is discussed in the next section.

# How to Choose Inputs/Set Variables

**Date Range of Metric Data to Examine**: The date range used for collecting metric data will depend to some extent on how well-defined the problem interval is. The objective is to choose a date range that will encompass not only the problem but a period of operation during which the problem did not exist. This date range will include, but be larger than, the next two intervals you will set. I often use a date range as far back as I have history or approximately a week if there is more than that available so that I can get a good handle on what was "normal" before the problem presented itself. I don't usually go further back than ten days because this gives me more data than I need although there may be times when this is desirable (see case study chapter 8 for an example of this). Another reason for subsetting the normalized metrics by the number of days back is that in some cases there is a month or more of AWR metrics and I usually don't need to look at all of them.

**Date Range for Problem Interval**: I will choose the date/time interval where the performance problem occurred only as wide as necessary in order to capture the problem. I don't want to cast my net too far and introduce unnecessary data "noise" into my analysis. Typically, I will use the date/time range provided by the client reporting the performance issue, unless a time-series analysis shows that the interval was likely bigger or smaller; in these cases, I'd rebuild the model using the adjusted date/time ranges.

If I'm not given an exact date time range for the problem, I usually select what I consider a slightly bigger time range and then narrow it in. For example, if I'm pretty sure the problem occurred on a specific day, I might use the entire day as the problem interval. I'll run the code using defaults for the parameters and a Metrics Aggregate View. Then I'll pick a metric from the Metrics Aggregate View that had the highest number of flagged metrics and the highest flag ratio and rerun the DOPA process using a Metrics Time-Series View to see the trend of when the metric went high. I can then use this information to narrow the date/time interval for the problem and take another pass at building the model. I usually wait to hear back from the client before making any judgments, but my analysis is usually spot-on.

**Date Range for Establishing Normals**: The date/time interval you select for establishing normal ranges will be a subset of the time interval you set for metric data collection (i.e., a subset of

Date Range of Metric Data to Examine). It will likely throw off the model if you randomly select a normal range interval, so the best interval to use is a date/time interval when the system was behaving normally. The bottom line is you want the normal range time interval to represent a time when the database was operating without problems so that the metrics will be truly representative of "normal." It is easier to determine a good interval when the problem has a clear starting time. If I am told it happened yesterday, for example, I would include all the metric data except for yesterday. If I am unsure of the time during which the problem occurred, I may use data from the weekend to establish normal values. Another way to discover a normal range interval is to look at the data from one or more time-series views and select a date/time range that appears normal from the data. For example, if Average Active Sessions were high during the problem interval, you could use an interval of low Average Active Sessions for the normal range interval. In cases where the normal range interval is not easy to determine, I might build the model a few times adjusting the normal range date/time interval until I obtained a set of flagged metrics that I could use for further analysis.

**Taxonomy**: As mentioned in the preceding text, I have two taxonomies currently implemented (infrastructure and Oracle). I use the infrastructure taxonomy as my default because this is the one I have spent the most time building out and refining.

The taxonomy is only as useful as it is complete and accurate. If many of the variables are listed as "other," it will be less useful than if all of the metrics are properly categorized. Use of the taxonomies allows you to bundle the metrics according to the taxonomy categories and thus determine the general category in which the performance problem is occurring (e.g., IO vs. CPU). This is particularly useful as a starting point for the analysis process. Once the type of problem is identified, it is possible to drill deeper with confidence that you are not missing important information or other problems. When the taxonomy is sufficiently developed, it is possible to gain an even better understanding of the problem by looking not only at the taxonomic groupings but the subcategory as well.

For example, if I'm seeing a lot of REDO metrics being flagged with high flag_ratios (i.e., more outside of normal range), then I might want to focus only on metrics that are in the Oracle taxonomy related to REDO and rerun the model subsetting on category = REDO as a refinement. Similarly, if analysis suggests to focus on a possible CPU-related problem, I can eliminate the "noise" created by the other metrics and look only at metrics related to the "CPU" category within the infrastructure taxonomy. Thus, the model will show the metrics that are most relevant to the problem area; this enables me to focus in on an area with a high degree of specificity.

**Metric sources**: I choose to look at all the metric sources on my first pass through a problem. Sometimes I exclude the dba_hist_latch source to get a faster model-building run. Also, with over 8,000 [often ill-documented] metrics in dba_hist_ latch, I find latches to be more difficult to interpret. Normally, I will do several iterations without the latch because it runs faster. I usually put latches back into the analysis once I have homed in on the problem for a final build of the model.

The beauty of the DOPA process is that it allows you to use the full arsenal of metrics available from Oracle. This is extremely useful for discovering the area of performance problems. But once you have identified the kind of problem, the DOPA process also enables you to limit the metric sources in order to focus in and gain a very detailed picture of the problem area.

As your familiarity with the different metrics increases, you may choose to focus on particular sources. For example, dba_hist_sysmetric_summary has a lot of workload metrics (i.e., <metric A> per transaction and <metric A>per second) which can be useful for deep-dive analysis. Similarly, dba_hist_osstat has metrics that derive mostly from the operating system, so in cases where operating system issues appear most pressing, one could focus attention on these metrics.

**Metric name**: My default on first pass through a
problem is to look at all metrics because I want my
first pass to give me a broad understanding of which
metrics are at play and what general area is having
problems. As stated previously, I can subset on a
single metric name or set of metric names using the
wildcard character, "%". I would typically subset on a
single metric name once I have narrowed in on the
problem area and want to do a deep-dive analysis
and get metric trending patterns using the Metrics
Time-Series View.

**Outlier sensitivity settings**: I use my default
computation for outliers unless I have a reason to
change it in subsequent runs. (My default is that
any value 1.5 times the IQR above Q3 or below
Q1 is identified as an outlier and removed—this
is covered in detail in Chapter 4.) Sometimes the
default IQR factor of 1.5 causes too many outliers
to be removed, so I will bump the IQR factor up
in order to limit the number of values that are
removed. When I don't want any outliers removed,
I can bump the IQR factor up to 1000. When less
outliers are removed, the normal ranges will be
broader and less values will be flagged as abnormal.
Conversely, if more outliers are removed, the
normal ranges will be narrower and more values will
be flagged outside of normal range. I will consider
constraining the removal of outliers when the model
produced swamps me with flagged metrics because
when there are too many flagged metrics, the
interpretation of the results is difficult.

One situation where I would want more outliers removed would be when I knew the typical absolute value ranges for a metric and the calculated normal ranges seemed unusually high. For example, I would expect to see ranges between 0 and 10 as normal for "Asynchronous Single-Block Read Latency" from dba_hist_sysmetric_summary. If I saw calculated values much higher than this for an upper limit on a particular run, I would want to either eliminate more outliers or find a different time interval that better represented a normal operation period. Note: If you are confident that the date/time interval used for the normal range calculations is representative of normal operating of the system, you won't need to tweak this parameter.

**Flagged values**: My default here is to choose to show flagged values only. One instance, however, where it is very helpful to see all values is when I want to look at a particular metric's trending over time. For this purpose, I will use the Metric Time-Series View and have all values displayed, not just the flagged metric values.

**Flag ratio**: Once again, the flag ratio is a measure of how many standard deviations from normal the metric value is. I start out using my default of zero for this variable so that I will see all metrics whose flag ratios are greater than zero, but there may be times I want to change this.

When the flag ratio is zero or close to zero, this means that the average value for the metric in the problem interval is just a little bit outside of normal range. The bigger the flag ratio, the further away from normal range the average metric value is. I would consider using a higher flag ratio if the model returns too many flagged metrics to easily analyze. By bumping the flag ratio up, I'll see less flagged metrics, but this is desirable since the metrics with the higher flag ratios are most likely to be the key influencers on the performance issue(s) being examined.

Once the subset variables are selected and you run the DOPA process, you will have a predictive model to guide you in your next steps. Because each performance case is unique, there are many factors that will influence your model-building choices. Again, you may iterate through the model-building process several times to arrive at a model that seems to be predictive/concise enough to guide further analysis. Following is a simple example of running the DOPA process including the results of the first run and how that predictive model directed the next steps of the analysis process.

# Example: Building the Model and Reporting

Here I will show a simple example of how the model is used to determine next steps based on the results of the first model. In Chapter 8 on case studies, there are a good number of real examples that give a more detailed picture of this process in action.

When beginning to investigate a performance issue, you can choose to start with a Category Count View which will help you understand the general areas where problems are occurring, or you can begin with Metrics Aggregate View which will give you the individual metrics that are most problematic. For this example, I chose to run the DOPA process and report using the Metrics Aggregate view. In this view, the table displays the metrics with the most flagged instances and highest flag ratio at the top of the list. Once I have that list, I go back and grab more detailed information for each of the top metrics and report that for the entire time interval. Figure 7-6 shows a portion of the Metrics Aggregate View which identifies dba_hist_osstat 'segment prealloc bytes' as the metric with the most flagged intervals and highest flag ratio. It was outside normal range for 10 of the 24 intervals.

| TAXONOMY_TYPE | CATEGORY | SUB_CATEGORY | STAT_SOURCE | METRIC_NAME | FLAG_COUNT | INTERVALS | AVG Flagged Values | LOWER_BOUND | UPPER_BOUND | FLAG_RATIO | FLAG_EVAL | AVG_All |
|---|---|---|---|---|---|---|---|---|---|---|---|---|
| Infrastructure | io | any | dba_hist_sysstat | physical reads bytes | 10 | 24 | 378136166 | 415190 | 1114112 | 1363.36 | ************* | 968271 |
| Infrastructure | any | any | dba_hist_sysstat | total number of slots | 9 | 24 | 18 | 2 | 8 | 4.75 | ************* | 4 |
| Infrastructure | memory | any | dba_hist_sysstat | switch current to new buffer | 8 | 24 | 552309 | 47144 | 65690 | 104.95 | ************* | 56417 |
| Infrastructure | io | any | dba_hist_sysstat | Batched IO slow jump count | 7 | 24 | 328 | 1 | 8 | 123.02 | ************* | 3 |
| Infrastructure | io | read | dba_hist_iostat_function | Direct Reads large_write_megabytes | 7 | 24 | 7664 | 241 | 483 | 118.7 | ************* | 362 |
| Infrastructure | io | any | dba_hist_sysstat | Batched IO buffer defrag count | 7 | 24 | 4124 | 1 | 110 | 100.1 | ************* | 30 |
| Infrastructure | io | concurrency | dba_hist_sysmetric_summary | CR Blocks Created Per Txn | 7 | 24 | 17 | 0 | 2 | 37.5 | ************* | 1 |
| Infrastructure | memory | any | dba_hist_sysstat | no buffer to keep pinned count | 7 | 24 | 1225 | 1 | 112 | 26.88 | ************* | 29 |
| Infrastructure | io | any | dba_hist_sysstat | deferred (CURRENT) block cleanout applications | 7 | 24 | 778135 | 45890 | 142500 | 26.32 | ************* | 94195 |
| Infrastructure | io | read | dba_hist_sysstat | transaction tables consistent reads - undo records applied | 7 | 24 | 72122 | 2 | 15767 | 10.75 | ************* | 5287 |
| Infrastructure | io | read | dba_hist_sysstat | rollbacks only - consistent read gets | 7 | 24 | 49749 | 160 | 17973 | 5.05 | ************* | 5399 |
| Infrastructure | io | any | dba_hist_sysstat | prefetched blocks aged out before use | 6 | 24 | 399869 | 14 | 1234 | 1093.05 | ************* | 505 |
| Infrastructure | io | read | dba_hist_iostat_function | Direct Writes small_read_megabytes | 6 | 24 | 202 | 1 | 3 | 332.22 | ************* | 2 |
| Infrastructure | io | read | dba_hist_iostat_function | Direct Writes large_read_megabytes | 6 | 24 | 5915 | 6 | 100 | 249.57 | ************* | 53 |
| Infrastructure | io | read | dba_hist_iostat_function | Direct Writes small_read_reqs | 6 | 24 | 3200 | 19 | 67 | 184.18 | ************* | 53 |

*Figure 7-6. Metrics Aggregate View example*

Now to take a closer look at that metric, I will run the code that produces the time-series view.

For this iteration of the model, I want to subset for just that metric and choose to see all values, not just the flagged values. An example of the output is in Figure 7-7.

***Figure 7-7.** Metrics Time-Series View is useful for deep-dive analysis of a particular area*

In Figure 7-8, I have graphed the same time-series data as shown in the table above so that the trend is more obvious.

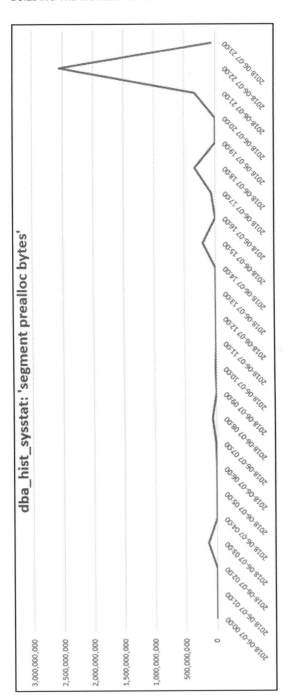

***Figure 7-8.*** *Metrics time-series graph example*

Often with the metrics time-series graphs, the periodicity of the metrics becomes readily apparent. For example, it is easy to see usage patterns of daytime workloads vs. nighttime workloads and/or usage patterns of weekend workloads vs. weekday workloads. Another example of periodicity would be periodic high workloads due to MView refreshes or other batch procedures. This would be an important observation because many metric anomalies can't be detected with constant [absolute value] thresholds. DOPA allows for a dynamic threshold for metric values since it is doing this comparison throughout the analysis.

Since I began with a Metrics Aggregate View for this analysis, I like to come back and confirm my analysis by looking at the Category Count View. As I said, it is possible to start the analysis with either of these views, but since I began with the one, I usually use the other to confirm the analysis. The Category Count View shows the taxonomic categories in which flags are occurring most frequently for a particular data set. To obtain a Category Count View, I run the model using the category count version of the code and subset again as I did for the Metrics Aggregate View. Figure 7-9 shows the Category Count View for the same data set used in the example described in the Metrics Aggregate View in Figure 7-1.

| TAXONOMY_TYPE | CATEGORY | CATEGORY_COUNT |
|---|---|---|
| Infrastructure | db | 12 |
| Infrastructure | io | 209 |
| Infrastructure | any | 29 |
| Infrastructure | cpu | 111 |
| Infrastructure | sql | 105 |
| Infrastructure | memory | 35 |
| Infrastructure | network | 14 |

**Figure 7-9.** *Category Count View, example table*

Even though you can see from this table that IO has the most flags, a graphical representation is effective in bringing home how great the difference is between IO and other areas of the infrastructure. I graphed the same category count results in a bar chart and that graph is shown in Figure 7-10. It is very easy to see from this graph that most of the flagged metrics are in the IO category.

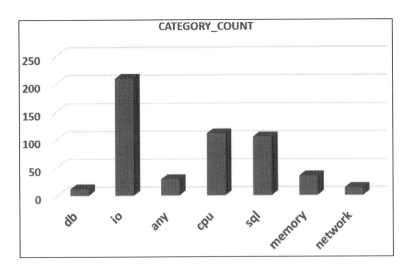

**Figure 7-10.** *Category Count View, example graph*

In the next example, a Category Count View was again used, but this time it was organized according to the Oracle taxonomy. The results are shown in Figure 7-11. The REDO area is the most flagged category with 64 flagged metrics. [NB: The larger number of metrics flagged in category ALL is an indicator that more work is needed to refine this taxonomy.]

| TAXONOMY_TYPE | CATEGORY | CATEGORY_COUNT |
|---|---|---|
| Oracle | ALL | 346 |
| Oracle | DBWR | 6 |
| Oracle | LGWR | 14 |
| Oracle | REDO | 64 |
| Oracle | UNDO | 14 |
| Oracle | PARSE | 14 |
| Oracle | OTHERS | 6 |
| Oracle | PL/SQL | 2 |
| Oracle | RESMGR | 4 |
| Oracle | LOCKING | 8 |
| Oracle | OS STAT | 6 |
| Oracle | STREAMS | 3 |
| Oracle | BACKGROUND | 4 |
| Oracle | CONNECTION | 1 |
| Oracle | DIRECT I/O | 18 |
| Oracle | COMPRESSION | 2 |
| Oracle | BUFFER CACHE | 3 |

*Figure 7-11.* *Category Count View using Oracle taxonomy*

# Summary

In this chapter, I have tried to give a plan of attack for how to implement the DOPA process in a general way. The starting point is usually either a Category Count View or a Metrics Aggregate View. The results of that first model will guide you in making choices for the inputs and view for further iterations of the model-building process. The end goal of these iterations is to allow you to focus in on problem areas and gain greater clarity regarding the performance issues. The tuning professional's skill comes into play in this process in that he/she will need to use good judgment to subset and interpret the data in order to discern a root cause and targeted solutions.

The next chapter provides multiple real examples with many nuanced uses of the DOPA process in action.

# PART III

# Case Studies and Further Applications

# CHAPTER 8

# Case Studies

In the previous chapter, I provided a framework for making the many decisions necessary when implementing the DOPA process. The discussion focused upon how you would choose to run the analysis, the various parameters, and views you would choose. In this chapter, I'll lead you through several real examples.

The case studies presented in this chapter show the DOPA process in action. They detail the analysis of historic AWR metrics and the identification of root cause(s) of real reported Oracle database performance problems. These represent just a sampling of the kinds of problems encountered by database tuning professionals, but taken together they demonstrate the dynamic nature of the DOPA process and its usefulness across problem types.

The DOPA process can provide valuable information and direct the tuning of multiple types of problems. I've listed in the following just a short list of the types of problems for which a dynamic analysis would prove very useful:

- Identifying source of performance bottlenecks:
  - IO
  - CPU
  - Memory
  - Network

- Identifying internal Oracle features involved in the performance issue:
    - Subsystems
    - Configuration
- Determining trends for thousands of metrics
- Identifying application issues:
    - Parsing
    - Workload
    - SQL tuning
- Failure detection:
    - ORA-600 errors
    - TEMP
    - PGA aggregate limit exceeded
- Analysis of metric normal ranges:
    - Threshold setting for monitoring

In any organization with mission-critical/important systems, it is essential to be able to quickly identify root causes of the issues and to react promptly by applying required corrections or tunings. As with any data analysis effort, context is key; without context for the issue you are analyzing, the results will have little meaning. In the context of database performance tuning (well-defined or not-so-well-defined issues), the unusual metric values flagged by the DOPA process will provide excellent input into the process of weaving the story behind the performance issue at hand.

With the approximately 11,000 metrics instrumented thus far in the DOPA process, there are about 2 million data points in a weeks' worth of AWR data (rolled up in 1-hour intervals). Since we're interested in performance bottlenecks, I designed the DOPA process to show only the metrics that are likely to be contributing to the problem. Likely, there will be many metrics that are unfamiliar to the new user of the DOPA process. While the metric names are usually informative as to what they are measuring, one might not be able to find a lot of Oracle documentation on a metric. Google is your friend to the extent that the metric is well documented, but not all of them are. Therefore, the DOPA process user will need to put on their expert hat, leveraging their knowledge of computer science and Oracle internals. The point is you will need to become familiar with a larger set of metrics than you are likely accustomed to. The DOPA process does not predetermine any metrics [although a future version will rank some well-known predictive metrics], and it is not designed to tell you specific metrics that are involved when a very specific performance issue is reported. Thus, it is the task of the DOPA process user to exercise good judgment and decide what metrics or problem areas to focus on for further analysis. The implementation of taxonomies is very helpful in this regard since they bundle the metrics into higher level categories for easier interpretation.

The analysis of the performance tuning expert is necessary to synthesize the results of the model produced by running the DOPA process for a given time interval. For example, a metric can be flagged by the DOPA process as out of normal range, but this condition could be a knock-on effect of another problem. For example, memory issues or poorly tuned SQL can surface in the metrics as IO problems (i.e., unusually high IO conditions can be a consequence of the real problem: low SGA memory or poorly tuned SQL). The user of the DOPA process will likely encounter this kind of behavior, as I did, time and time again. The model produced by the DOPA process is a very effective tool, but it must be used skillfully by the tuning professional, who must take the objective information it affords to convey the metrics-based "story" that best expresses the performance issue at hand.

For the following case studies, I had access to production Oracle instances that contained one weeks' worth of historic performance metrics in the DBA_HIST views (in some cases, up to one month's worth of data). Each case represents a real production performance incident. Each was solved in the "heat of battle" using the DOPA process.

# Case Studies

In each of the case studies, I have answered the following questions to provide you with a framework for understanding the problem and a guide for the thought process I used in resolving the issue using the DOPA predictive model to guide me:

What was the user's complaint? How did the problem manifest? Error messages?

What type of analysis did I run with the DOPA code? Metrics flagged, interesting patterns?

What action did I take to resolve the issue?

Why is this case particularly interesting?

What impact did the metrics analysis bring?

# Case #1: Basic Example Showing How DOPA Process Identifies a SQL Problem

*What was the user's complaint? How did the problem manifest? Error messages?*

The application had poor performance during a particular time interval. Users asked us to check to see if there were backups or other processes occurring on the database that might be impacting their application.

What type of analysis did I run with the DOPA process? Metrics flagged, interesting patterns?

I ran my code using a Metrics Aggregate View for the problem interval since the users provided a well-defined interval. Flagged metrics identified high values for several TEMP tablespace-related metrics as shown in Figure 8-1.

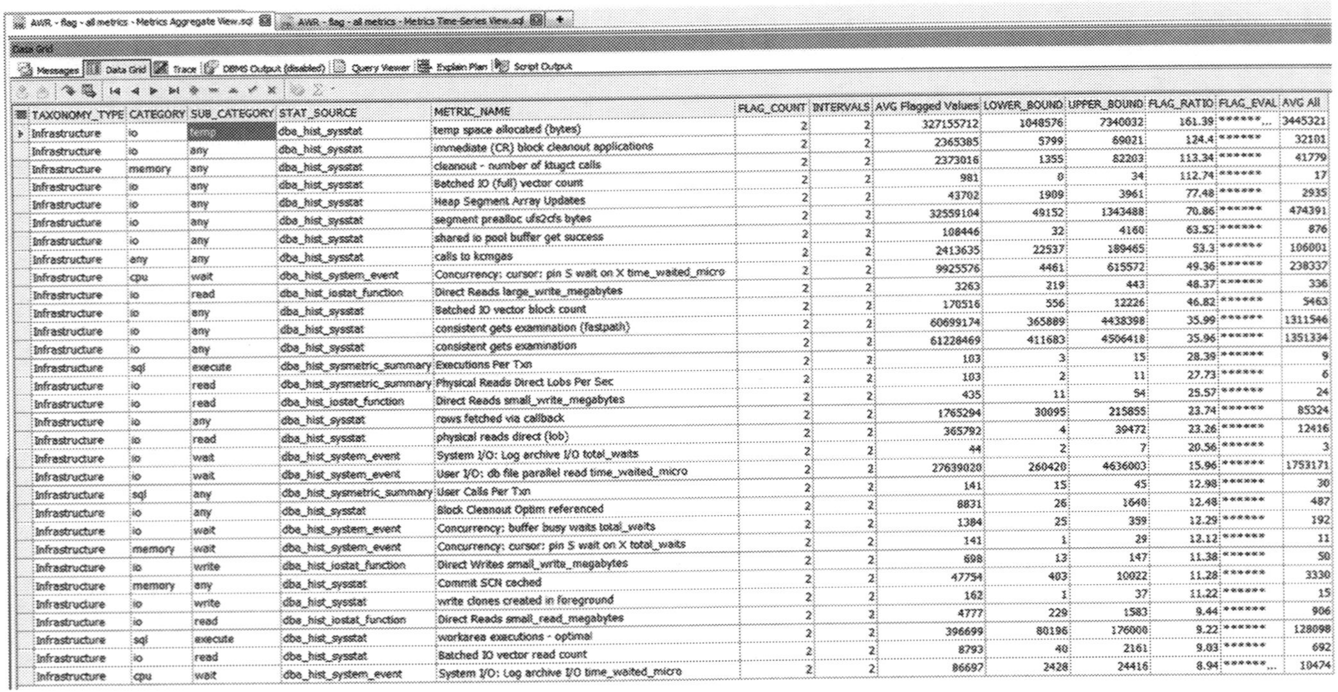


| TAXONOMY_TYPE | CATEGORY | SUB_CATEGORY | STAT_SOURCE | METRIC_NAME | FLAG_COUNT | INTERVALS | AVG Flagged Values | LOWER_BOUND | UPPER_BOUND | FLAG_RATIO | FLAG_EVAL | AVG All |
|---|---|---|---|---|---|---|---|---|---|---|---|---|
| Infrastructure | io | temp | dba_hist_sysstat | temp space allocated (bytes) | 2 | 2 | 327155712 | 1048576 | 7340032 | 161.39 | ******... | 3445321 |
| Infrastructure | io | any | dba_hist_sysstat | immediate (CR) block cleanout applications | 2 | 2 | 2365385 | 5799 | 69021 | 124.4 | ****** | 32101 |
| Infrastructure | memory | any | dba_hist_sysstat | cleanout - number of ktugct calls | 2 | 2 | 2373016 | 1355 | 82203 | 113.34 | ****** | 41779 |
| Infrastructure | io | any | dba_hist_sysstat | Batched IO (full) vector count | 2 | 2 | 981 | 0 | 34 | 112.74 | ****** | 17 |
| Infrastructure | io | any | dba_hist_sysstat | Heap Segment Array Updates | 2 | 2 | 43702 | 1909 | 3961 | 77.48 | ****** | 2935 |
| Infrastructure | io | any | dba_hist_sysstat | segment prealloc ufs2cfs bytes | 2 | 2 | 32559104 | 49152 | 1343488 | 70.86 | ****** | 474391 |
| Infrastructure | io | any | dba_hist_sysstat | shared io pool buffer get success | 2 | 2 | 108446 | 32 | 4160 | 63.52 | ****** | 876 |
| Infrastructure | any | any | dba_hist_sysstat | calls to kcmgas | 2 | 2 | 2413635 | 22537 | 189465 | 53.3 | ****** | 106001 |
| Infrastructure | cpu | wait | dba_hist_system_event | Concurrency: cursor: pin S wait on X time_waited_micro | 2 | 2 | 9925576 | 4461 | 615572 | 49.36 | ****** | 238337 |
| Infrastructure | io | read | dba_hist_iostat_function | Direct Reads large_write_megabytes | 2 | 2 | 3263 | 319 | 443 | 48.37 | ****** | 336 |
| Infrastructure | io | any | dba_hist_sysstat | Batched IO vector block count | 2 | 2 | 170516 | 556 | 12226 | 46.82 | ****** | 5463 |
| Infrastructure | io | any | dba_hist_sysstat | consistent gets examination (fastpath) | 2 | 2 | 60699174 | 365889 | 4438398 | 35.99 | ****** | 1311546 |
| Infrastructure | io | any | dba_hist_sysstat | consistent gets examination | 2 | 2 | 61228469 | 411683 | 4506418 | 35.96 | ****** | 1351334 |
| Infrastructure | sql | execute | dba_hist_sysmetric_summary | Executions Per Txn | 2 | 2 | 103 | 3 | 15 | 28.39 | ****** | 9 |
| Infrastructure | io | read | dba_hist_sysmetric_summary | Physical Reads Direct Lobs Per Sec | 2 | 2 | 103 | 2 | 11 | 27.73 | ****** | 6 |
| Infrastructure | io | read | dba_hist_iostat_function | Direct Reads small_write_megabytes | 2 | 2 | 435 | 11 | 54 | 25.57 | ****** | 24 |
| Infrastructure | io | any | dba_hist_sysstat | rows fetched via callback | 2 | 2 | 1765294 | 30095 | 215855 | 23.74 | ****** | 85324 |
| Infrastructure | io | read | dba_hist_sysstat | physical reads direct (lob) | 2 | 2 | 365792 | 4 | 39472 | 23.26 | ****** | 12416 |
| Infrastructure | io | wait | dba_hist_system_event | System I/O: Log archive I/O total_waits | 2 | 2 | 44 | 2 | 7 | 20.56 | ****** | 3 |
| Infrastructure | io | wait | dba_hist_system_event | User I/O: db file parallel read time_waited_micro | 2 | 2 | 27639020 | 260420 | 4636003 | 15.96 | ****** | 1753171 |
| Infrastructure | sql | any | dba_hist_sysmetric_summary | User Calls Per Txn | 2 | 2 | 141 | 15 | 45 | 12.98 | ****** | 30 |
| Infrastructure | io | any | dba_hist_sysstat | Block Cleanout Optim referenced | 2 | 2 | 8831 | 26 | 1640 | 12.48 | ****** | 487 |
| Infrastructure | io | wait | dba_hist_system_event | Concurrency: buffer busy waits total_waits | 2 | 2 | 1384 | 25 | 359 | 12.29 | ****** | 192 |
| Infrastructure | memory | wait | dba_hist_system_event | Concurrency: cursor: pin S wait on X total_waits | 2 | 2 | 141 | 1 | 29 | 12.12 | ****** | 11 |
| Infrastructure | io | write | dba_hist_iostat_function | Direct Writes small_write_megabytes | 2 | 2 | 698 | 13 | 147 | 11.38 | ****** | 50 |
| Infrastructure | memory | any | dba_hist_sysstat | Commit SCN cached | 2 | 2 | 47754 | 403 | 10022 | 11.28 | ****** | 3330 |
| Infrastructure | io | write | dba_hist_sysstat | write clones created in foreground | 2 | 2 | 162 | 1 | 37 | 11.22 | ****** | 15 |
| Infrastructure | io | read | dba_hist_iostat_function | Direct Reads small_read_megabytes | 2 | 2 | 4777 | 229 | 1583 | 9.44 | ****** | 906 |
| Infrastructure | sql | execute | dba_hist_sysstat | workarea executions - optimal | 2 | 2 | 396699 | 80196 | 176000 | 9.22 | ****** | 128098 |
| Infrastructure | io | read | dba_hist_sysstat | Batched IO vector read count | 2 | 2 | 8793 | 40 | 2161 | 9.03 | ****** | 692 |
| Infrastructure | cpu | wait | dba_hist_system_event | System I/O: Log archive I/O time_waited_micro | 2 | 2 | 86697 | 2428 | 24416 | 8.94 | ******... | 10474 |

**Figure 8-1.** *Flagged metrics reveal high values for several TEMP tablespace-related metrics*

Since TEMP usage will come from SQL and sometimes SQL can be tuned to reduce TEMP consumption, I looked at the ASH during the time interval during which the problem was occurring to find the top TEMP-producing SQL. I ran that SQL through the SQL Tuning Advisor and examined the SQL Stats and ASH for the SQL [it took 8 minutes to run, returning 300,000 rows (1000 at a time) over the wide area network; session elapsed time was 30 minutes]. SQL Tuning Advisor suggested a parallel SQL Profile at ~60% improvement. In this case the root cause was not really TEMP consumption, but rather the fact that the query was running over the WAN (app server in the UK with the database in the United States) with a low array fetch size.

*What did you do to resolve the issue?*

My resolution included the following actions:

1) Increasing the array fetch size

2) Relocating app server to same local area network with the database

3) Tuning using parallel SQL Profile

*Why is this case particularly interesting?*

This example shows how a problem area (high TEMP-consuming SQL) was quickly identified by the DOPA process. It also shows the importance of rightly interpreting that information. Clearly, the tuning expert must be able to make the jump from raw fact (high TEMP consumption) to a likely cause(s).

*What impact did the metrics analysis bring?* The DOPA process quickly identified one and only one problem area. Tuning attention was then directed to that problematic area. A deep-dive analysis at that point efficiently and effectively identified the root cause.

# Case #2: Basic Example of How the DOPA Process Identified a Configuration Problem

*What was user complaint? How did the problem manifest? Error messages?*

Client reported performance degradation during a massive data load. There was a three-hour window during which this program ran.

What type of analysis did I run with the DOPA code? Metrics flagged, interesting patterns?

I ran the DOPA analysis using a Category Count View and the Oracle taxonomy for the problem interval.

The Category Count View, shown in Figure 8-2, shows REDO and IO metrics were the taxonomic areas most often flagged as abnormal. This would likely indicate a configuration problem as the cause of performance degradation.

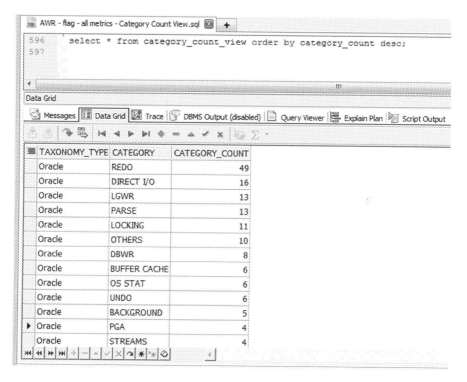

***Figure 8-2.*** *Category Count View showing high numbers of flags in REDO and DIRECT I/O probably indicative of a configuration problem*

To get more detail, I ran the DOPA model again, this time using the Metrics Aggregate View. This view is shown in Figure 8-3. The Metrics Aggregate View shows the individual metrics with the most flagged values. In this instance, seven of the top nine metrics are REDO-related metrics, confirming that a REDO configuration problem is most likely the root problem.

| TAXONOMY_TYPE | CATEGORY | SUB_CATEGORY | STAT_SOURCE | METRIC_NAME | FLAG_COUNT | INTERVALS | AVG | Flagged Values | LOWER_BOUND | UPPER_BOUND | FLAG_RATIO | FLAG_EVAL | AVG All |
|---|---|---|---|---|---|---|---|---|---|---|---|---|---|
| Oracle | REDO | COUNT | dba_hist_sysstat | redo write size count (ref) | 4 | 4 | | 11910 | 1 | 23 | 1264.57 | ********** | 4 |
| Oracle | REDO | ALL | dba_hist_sysstat | redo size | 4 | 4 | | 338842S936 | 3784396 | 65451602 | 1247.46 | ********** | 11231256 |
| Oracle | REDO | WORKLOAD | dba_hist_sysmetric_summary | Redo Generated Per Sec | 4 | 4 | | 9338544 | 1036 | 181194 | 1237.62 | ********** | 3132 |
| Oracle | DBWR | ALL | dba_hist_iostat_function | DBWR large_write_reqs | 4 | 4 | | 1949910 | 9 | 381 | 1236.68 | ********** | 66 |
| Oracle | REDO | ALL | dba_hist_sysstat | redo blocks written | 4 | 4 | | 68418608 | 8769 | 133800 | 1235.4 | ********** | 2325 |
| Oracle | DBWR | ALL | dba_hist_iostat_function | DBWR large_write_ megabytes | 4 | 4 | | 24364 | 1 | 47 | 1234.36 | ********** | 8 |
| Oracle | REDO | ALL | dba_hist_sysstat | redo KB read | 4 | 4 | | 34164013 | 3857 | 69823 | 1261.35 | ********** | 13063 |
| Oracle | REDO | WORKLOAD | dba_hist_sysmetric_summary | Redo Generated Per TXn | 4 | 4 | | 6906403 | 5554 | 23421 | 1123.75 | ********** | 1172 |
| Oracle | REDO | ALL | dba_hist_sysstat | redo entries | 4 | 4 | | 63553069 | 6537 | 140721 | 1087.86 | ********** | 24503 |
| Oracle | ALL | TIME | dba_hist_system_event | System I/O: db file async I/O submit time_worked_micro | 4 | 4 | | 443731663 | 43411 | 1101070 | 991.24 | ********** | 207981 |
| Oracle | REDO | COUNT | dba_hist_sysstat | redo write size count ( 512KB) | 4 | 4 | | 10241 | 1 | 26 | 928.66 | ********** | 4 |
| Oracle | ALL | ALL | dba_hist_sysstat | physical writes from cache | 4 | 4 | | 17981723 | 1308 | 48200 | 885.52 | ********** | 7922 |
| Oracle | ALL | TIME | dba_hist_sysstat | change write time | 4 | 4 | | 146823 | 28 | 440 | 841.28 | ........... | 92 |

*Figure 8-3. Metrics Aggregate View showing likely configuration issue*

I used the objects that generated the most block changes (source: DBA_HIST_SEG_STAT and DBA_HIST_SEG_STAT_OBJ) as a "surrogate metric" to discover the SQL causing the massive REDO. Figure 8-4 shows the results of this search—it reveals that a single-row array insert of about 78 million rows (20,000 records at a time) which took about 7.5 seconds per execution and required approximately 8 hours of processing time was the problem.

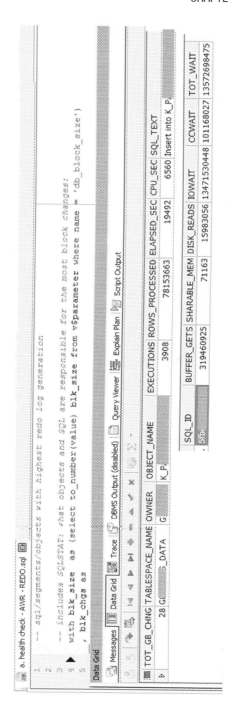

***Figure 8-4.*** *Example where the surrogate metric of block changes is used to get the likely SQL causing the massive REDO*

The next step I took was to look at the wait events for this SQL; I did this using a custom query against the ASH. I could see from this query that log file switching and IO delays were contributing to the issue. This analysis confirmed that the REDO configuration was a major part of the problem.

The actual configuration problem shows up in the following Log Switch Frequency Map, shown in Figure 8-5, which reveals that log file switching was excessively high during the problem interval.

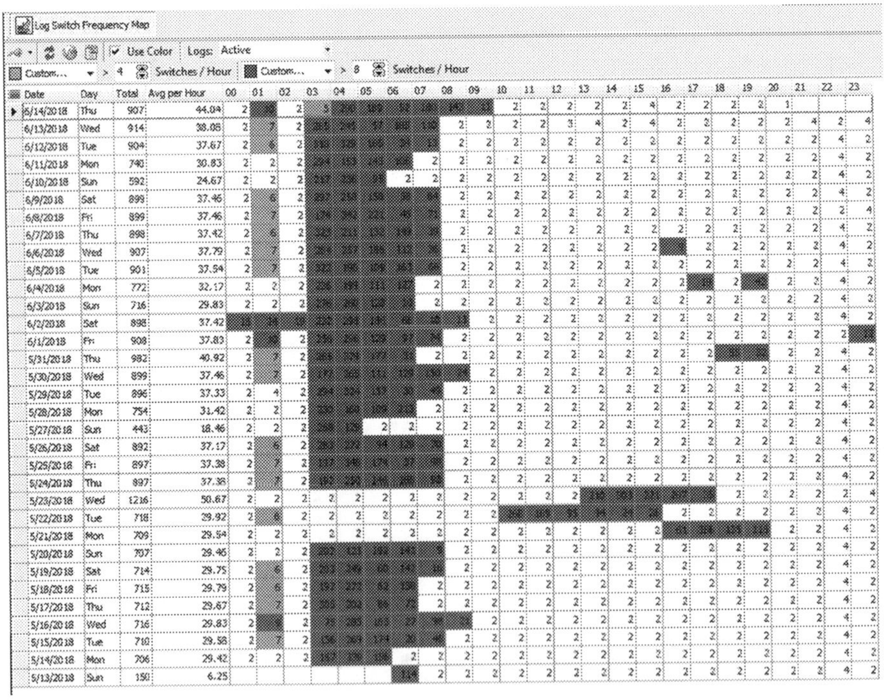

*Figure 8-5. Log Switch Frequency Map confirming a configuration problem*

Confirming the size of the REDO Log files as in Figure 8-6, I concluded that the solution was to increase the REDO log file sizes to at least 2 GB each.

| Group | Thread | Sequence | Size | Members | Archived | Status | First Change | First Time |
|-------|--------|----------|------|---------|----------|--------|--------------|------------|
| 1 | 1 | 135917 | 200 MB | 2 | YES | INACTIVE | 14964355758599 | 6/14/2018 8:00:54 PM |
| 2 | 1 | 135918 | 200 MB | 2 | NO | CURRENT | 14964355762283 | 6/14/2018 8:30:54 PM |
| 3 | 1 | 135915 | 200 MB | 2 | YES | INACTIVE | 14964348002553 | 6/14/2018 7:00:55 PM |
| 4 | 1 | 135916 | 200 MB | 2 | YES | INACTIVE | 14964348005734 | 6/14/2018 7:30:52 PM |

***Figure 8-6.*** *Confirming the size of the REDO Log files*

Advice from ADDM was consistent with my conclusion since it recommended an increase in the SGA. Since IO waits were also at play, this action will be taken at the earliest convenience (database restart required). The ADDM report excerpt is in Figure 8-7.

```
Finding 3: Undersized SGA
Impact is .19 active sessions, 13.03% of total activity.
---------------------------------------------------------------
The SGA was inadequately sized, causing additional I/O or hard parses.
The value of parameter "sga_target" was "3072 M" during the analysis period.

   Recommendation 1: Database Configuration
   Estimated benefit is .19 active sessions, 12.71% of total activity.
   ---------------------------------------------------------------
   Action
      Increase the size of the SGA by setting the parameter "sga_target" to
      3840 M.

Symptoms That Led to the Finding:
---------------------------------------------------------------
   Wait class "User I/O" was consuming significant database time.
   Impact is .44 active sessions, 29.61% of total activity.
   Hard parsing of SQL statements was consuming significant database time.
   Impact is .14 active sessions, 9.17% of total activity.
```

***Figure 8-7.*** *ADDM report excerpt*

Further iterations of the DOPA process showed high values for index leaf node splits.

*What action did I take to resolve the issue?*

The actions taken to address the performance problem are as follows:

Increase REDO log file sizes.

Increase the size of the SGA.

To address the problem of high values for index leaf node splits, I suggested to the client that they disable the indexes during the load.

*Why is this case particularly interesting?*

*Leaf node splits* is a metric implemented in AWR and evaluated as part of the DOPA process, but I have never seen it in any other small model approach. It was noteworthy that the DOPA process identified it as a problem in this analysis. It is quite likely that this is a problem that occurs, but is overlooked by other tools that fail to consider this metric.

REDO and IO issues as well as the index issues were immediately flagged in this analysis and led to a much richer root-cause analysis. As noted in the preceding text, inclusion of all metrics prevented important observations from being missed. Once the problem area was discovered using the DOPA process, a more in-depth analysis could be performed using other tools. For example, a little bit of further digging showed that the resource manager was kicking in as highlighted in Figure 8-8.

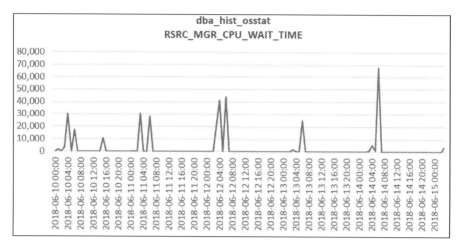

***Figure 8-8.*** *Resource manager metrics from dba_hist_osstat*

The high values for the metric dba_hist_osstat: "SRC_MGR_CPU_ WAIT_TIME" pointed me to check if the resource manager was kicking in during the maintenance window activities. It turns out that it was occurring during the problem interval. To address this, the solutions include

1) Maintenance window should be moved to a period of less activity.

2) The resource management plan should be dialed back.

3) Possibly also the instance/machine needs more CPU.

*What impact did the metrics analysis bring?*

Using DOPA process as a first step in the analysis enabled me to positively identify the area of concern based on the flagged metrics. I was able to then use small model tools to zoom in on the problem area with great precision. Having done a comprehensive analysis first, I could be confident that important observations were not being overlooked and that all problem areas were addressed.

# Case #3: CPU Problem Caused by SQL Execution

*What was the user's complaint? How did the problem manifest? Error messages?*

The client complained that a specific query configured in a monitoring tool was throwing alerts—"ORA-01013: user requested cancel of current operation." They reported that normal query execution time was usually much less than 60 seconds and that the application would error out if >60 seconds.

Client received the alerts on June 14–16 and also 18–20. The request read, "Please check and let us know is there any Performance issue at the database end."

Another analyst had previously looked at the problem and recommended that the client modify the query with a parallel hint. This change was made by the client, but did not resolve the problem. In fact, it magnified the problem.

What type of analysis did I run with the DOPA code? Metrics flagged, interesting patterns?

I began the analysis by running the DOPA code using the Metrics Category Count View to gain a high-level picture of the situation. As shown in Figure 8-9, an overwhelming number of the flagged metrics were IO- and CPU-related metrics.

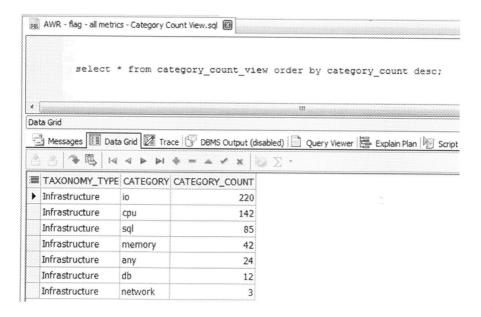

*Figure 8-9.* *Metrics Category Count View showing a predominance of IO- and CPU-related metrics flagged*

A second iteration of the DOPA process, using the Metrics Aggregate View, gave a more detailed view. In the Metrics Aggregate View, shown in Figure 8-10, I can see a number of specific CPU-related metrics that are high. These are indicated by arrows.

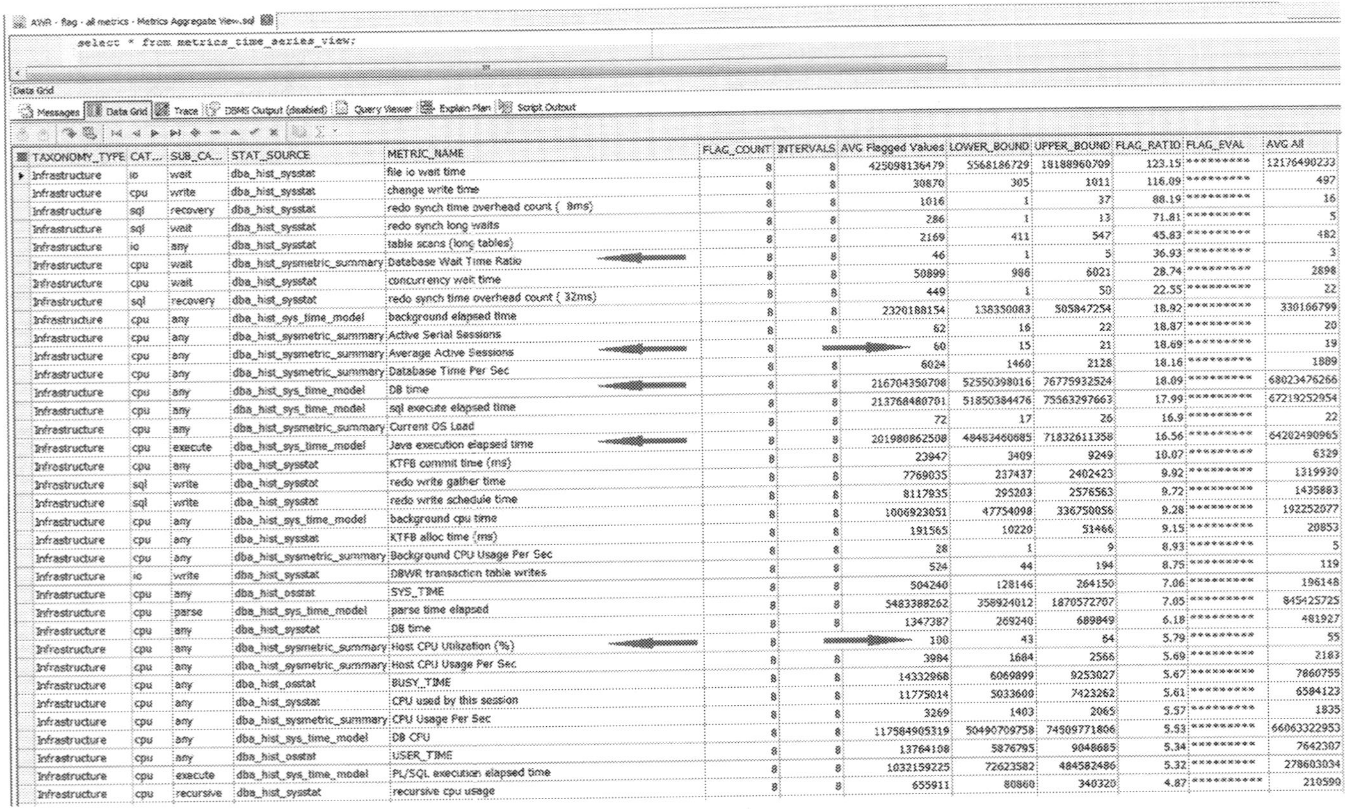


| TAXONOMY_TYPE | CAT... | SUB_CA... | STAT_SOURCE | METRIC_NAME | FLAG_COUNT | INTERVALS | AVG Flagged Values | LOWER_BOUND | UPPER_BOUND | FLAG_RATIO | FLAG_EVAL | AVG All |
|---|---|---|---|---|---|---|---|---|---|---|---|---|
| Infrastructure | io | wait | dba_hist_sysstat | file io wait time | 8 | 8 | 4250981364 79 | 5568186729 | 18188960709 | 123.15 | ********* | 12176490233 |
| Infrastructure | cpu | write | dba_hist_sysstat | change write time | 8 | 8 | 30870 | 305 | 1011 | 116.09 | ********* | 497 |
| Infrastructure | sql | recovery | dba_hist_sysstat | redo synch time overhead count ( 8ms) | 8 | 8 | 1016 | 1 | 37 | 88.19 | ********* | 16 |
| Infrastructure | sql | wait | dba_hist_sysstat | redo synch long waits | 8 | 8 | 286 | 1 | 13 | 71.81 | ********* | 5 |
| Infrastructure | io | any | dba_hist_sysstat | table scans (long tables) | 8 | 8 | 2169 | 411 | 547 | 45.83 | ********* | 482 |
| Infrastructure | cpu | wait | dba_hist_sysmetric_summary | Database Wait Time Ratio | 8 | 8 | 46 | 1 | 5 | 36.93 | ********* | 3 |
| Infrastructure | cpu | wait | dba_hist_sysstat | concurrency wait time | 8 | 8 | 50899 | 986 | 6021 | 28.74 | ********* | 2898 |
| Infrastructure | sql | recovery | dba_hist_sysstat | redo synch time overhead count ( 32ms) | 8 | 8 | 449 | 1 | 50 | 22.55 | ********* | 22 |
| Infrastructure | cpu | any | dba_hist_sys_time_model | background elapsed time | 8 | 8 | 2320188154 | 138350083 | 505847254 | 18.92 | ********* | 330166799 |
| Infrastructure | cpu | any | dba_hist_sysmetric_summary | Active Serial Sessions | 8 | 8 | 62 | 16 | 22 | 18.87 | ********* | 20 |
| Infrastructure | cpu | any | dba_hist_sysmetric_summary | Average Active Sessions | 8 | | 60 | 15 | 21 | 18.69 | ********* | 19 |
| Infrastructure | cpu | any | dba_hist_sysmetric_summary | Database Time Per Sec | 8 | 8 | 6024 | 1460 | 2128 | 18.16 | ********* | 1889 |
| Infrastructure | cpu | any | dba_hist_sys_time_model | DB time | 8 | 8 | 216704350708 | 52550398016 | 76775932524 | 18.09 | ********* | 68023476266 |
| Infrastructure | cpu | any | dba_hist_sys_time_model | sql execute elapsed time | 8 | 8 | 213768480701 | 51850384476 | 75563297663 | 17.99 | ********* | 67219252954 |
| Infrastructure | cpu | any | dba_hist_sysmetric_summary | Current OS Load | 8 | 8 | 72 | 17 | 26 | 16.9 | ********* | 22 |
| Infrastructure | cpu | execute | dba_hist_sys_time_model | Java execution elapsed time | 8 | 8 | 201980862508 | 48483460685 | 71832611358 | 16.56 | ********* | 64202490965 |
| Infrastructure | cpu | any | dba_hist_sysstat | KTFB commit time (ms) | 8 | 8 | 23947 | 3409 | 9249 | 10.07 | ********* | 6329 |
| Infrastructure | sql | write | dba_hist_sysstat | redo write gather time | 8 | 8 | 7769035 | 237437 | 2402423 | 9.92 | ********* | 1319930 |
| Infrastructure | sql | write | dba_hist_sysstat | redo write schedule time | 8 | 8 | 8117935 | 295203 | 2576563 | 9.72 | ********* | 1435883 |
| Infrastructure | cpu | any | dba_hist_sys_time_model | background cpu time | 8 | 8 | 1006923051 | 47754098 | 336750056 | 9.28 | ********* | 192252077 |
| Infrastructure | cpu | any | dba_hist_sysstat | KTFB alloc time (ms) | 8 | 8 | 191565 | 10220 | 51466 | 9.15 | ********* | 20853 |
| Infrastructure | cpu | any | dba_hist_sysmetric_summary | Background CPU Usage Per Sec | 8 | 8 | 28 | 1 | 9 | 8.93 | ********* | 5 |
| Infrastructure | io | write | dba_hist_sysstat | DBWR transaction table writes | 8 | 8 | 524 | 44 | 194 | 8.75 | ********* | 119 |
| Infrastructure | cpu | any | dba_hist_osstat | SYS_TIME | 8 | 8 | 504240 | 128146 | 264150 | 7.06 | ********* | 196148 |
| Infrastructure | cpu | parse | dba_hist_sys_time_model | parse time elapsed | 8 | 8 | 5483388262 | 358924012 | 1870572707 | 7.05 | ********* | 845425725 |
| Infrastructure | cpu | any | dba_hist_sysstat | DB time | 8 | 8 | 1347387 | 269240 | 689849 | 6.18 | ********* | 481927 |
| Infrastructure | cpu | any | dba_hist_sysmetric_summary | Host CPU Utilization (%) | 8 | | 100 | 43 | 64 | 5.79 | ********* | 55 |
| Infrastructure | cpu | any | dba_hist_sysmetric_summary | Host CPU Usage Per Sec | 8 | 8 | 3984 | 1684 | 2566 | 5.69 | ********* | 2183 |
| Infrastructure | cpu | any | dba_hist_osstat | BUSY_TIME | 8 | 8 | 14332968 | 6069899 | 9253027 | 5.67 | ********* | 7860755 |
| Infrastructure | cpu | any | dba_hist_sysstat | CPU used by this session | 8 | 8 | 11775014 | 5033600 | 7423262 | 5.61 | ********* | 6584123 |
| Infrastructure | cpu | any | dba_hist_sysmetric_summary | CPU Usage Per Sec | 8 | 8 | 3269 | 1403 | 2065 | 5.57 | ********* | 1835 |
| Infrastructure | cpu | any | dba_hist_sys_time_model | DB CPU | 8 | 8 | 117584905319 | 50490709758 | 74509771806 | 5.53 | ********* | 66063322953 |
| Infrastructure | cpu | any | dba_hist_osstat | USER_TIME | 8 | 8 | 13764108 | 5876795 | 9048685 | 5.34 | ********* | 7642307 |
| Infrastructure | cpu | execute | dba_hist_sys_time_model | PL/SQL execution elapsed time | 8 | 8 | 1032159225 | 72623582 | 484582486 | 5.32 | ********* | 278603034 |
| Infrastructure | cpu | recursive | dba_hist_sysstat | recursive cpu usage | 8 | 8 | 655911 | 80860 | 340320 | 4.87 | ********** | 210590 |

***Figure 8-10.*** *Metrics Aggregate View*

I was able to do a deeper-dive analysis by looking at a Metrics Time-Series View. Using the Metrics Time-Series View, I focused in on dba_hist_sysmetric_summary: "Host CPU Utilization (%)" (shown in Figure 8-11) and could see that the CPU had been pegged for a long time. When this happens, all waits are inflated because of the wait for CPU (see "Database Wait Time Ratio" graph in Figure 8-12).

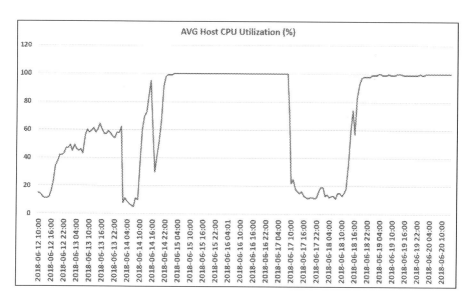

***Figure 8-11.*** *Host CPU Utilization graph*

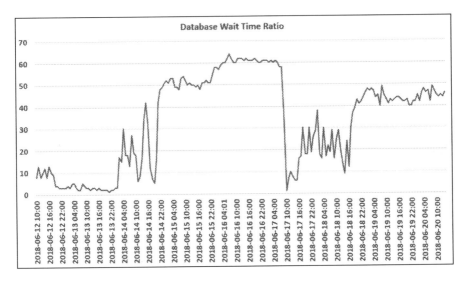

***Figure 8-12.***  *Database Wait Time Ratio graph*

Additional information gathered revealed the following:

```
cpu_count = 40
SBR latency metrics look good.
Top SQL from ADDM:  6da7h2v0b1v8z Findings from ADDM:
```
**98% for Java execution.**
```
1- Statistics Finding
---------------------

   Table "CODS_USER_SS_PROD"."SS_CXSMILES_EXACT_SEARCH" was not
   analyzed.
```

Based on all the information, I determined that CPU was the root cause of the issue for the fluctuations in monitoring and that the problem would likely persist until the CPU situation was brought under control. I was confident that it wasn't a capacity issue and that performance would improve once the SQL was tuned.

*What action did I take to resolve the issue?*

1. Implement a custom SQL Profile fixing the execution plan to the faster PHV (3051534597).

2. Monitor CPU situation and revisit if no improvement.

*Why is this case particularly interesting?*

The first analyst that looked at this problem recommended that the client modify the query with a parallel hint. This change was made by the client, but did not resolve the problem. In fact, it magnified the problem. In making this change, the analyst was treating the symptom and not the problem.

The DOPA process, a comprehensive metrics-based analysis, identified not only the CPU issue but also the impact of the CPU issue on various wait times. This is a great example of how the expertise of the analyst is critical for the interpretation of the raw data. In this case, the long wait times were a result of slow processing due to high CPU consumption, not the problem to be fixed. Throwing hardware at the problem *might* help, but it is unlikely to solve the problem.

What impact did the metrics analysis bring?

The comprehensive analysis enabled accurate identification of the problem and the information necessary to discern between cause and effect.

In follow-up evaluation after the fix, Figure 8-13 shows that the CPU situation has returned to normal. The long-duration high CPU condition of the server remained under control after implementing the custom manual SQL Profile.

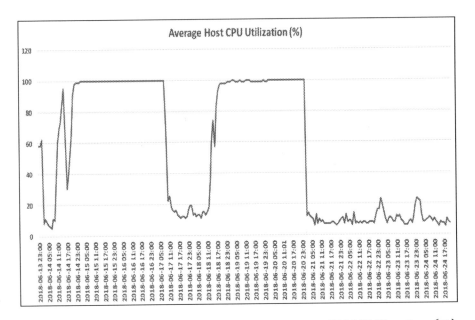

***Figure 8-13.*** *CPU graph showing Average Host CPU Utilization (%) returned to normal after the fix*

# Case #4: Example Where the DOPA Process Was Used to Detail Problem Areas

*What was the user's complaint? How did the problem manifest? Error messages?*

Performance was reported to be slow on a particular database instance, and the client reported application level server busy errors (no "ORA" errors reported).

This is a database application that is hosted in the UK but has US users as well. The problem got worse as US users began to connect to the application and gradually eased when UK users logged off. The time period during which this happened most was every day between 10:00 and 15:00, for different users at different sites.

What type of analysis did I run with the DOPA code? Metrics flagged, interesting patterns?

Since the problem occurred only during the week, I took my normal ranges from the weekend, using the same time interval: 10:00–15:00.

I went first to the Metrics Aggregate View looking only at dba_hist_sysmetric_summary metrics (since this source is loaded with transactional related metrics). Figure 8-14 shows the model produced:

| METRIC_NAME | FLAG COUNT | INTER-VALS | AVG Flagged Values | LOWER BOUND | UPPER BOUND | FLAG RATIO | AVG All |
|---|---|---|---|---|---|---|---|
| Current Open Cursors Count | 6 | 6 | 8,464 | 1,902 | 1,977 | 248 | 1,954 |
| Current Logons Count | 6 | 6 | 2,202 | 482 | 505 | 207 | 498 |
| Session Count | 6 | 6 | 2,223 | 495 | 520 | 203 | 512 |
| Total Table Scans Per Sec | 6 | 6 | 384 | 4 | 22 | 61 | 16 |
| Network Traffic Volume Per Sec | 6 | 6 | 4,820,904 | 231,550 | 496,970 | 59 | 378,184 |
| Executions Per Sec | 6 | 6 | 1,476 | 24 | 95 | 55 | 75 |
| Redo Writes Per Sec | 6 | 6 | 46 | 2 | 5 | 51 | 4 |
| Open Cursors Per Sec | 6 | 6 | 1,146 | 17 | 82 | 50 | 60 |
| Physical Reads Direct Lobs Per Sec | 6 | 6 | 42 | 0 | 4 | 38 | 2 |
| User Commits Per Sec | 6 | 6 | 34 | 1 | 3 | 38 | 3 |
| User Transaction Per Sec | 6 | 6 | 34 | 1 | 3 | 38 | 3 |
| Enqueue Requests Per Sec | 6 | 6 | 305 | 26 | 47 | 37 | 40 |
| User Calls Per Sec | 6 | 6 | 7,245 | 7 | 677 | 33 | 406 |
| Total Parse Count Per Sec | 6 | 6 | 99 | 4 | 14 | 27 | 10 |
| Recursive Calls Per Sec | 6 | 6 | 664 | 32 | 95 | 26 | 77 |
| Physical Read Bytes Per Sec | 6 | 6 | 7,834,320 | 231,734 | 1,471,471 | 16 | 1,015,168 |
| Physical Reads Per Sec | 6 | 6 | 956 | 28 | 180 | 16 | 124 |

***Figure 8-14.*** *Case Study - UKPRD835 - Metrics Aggregate View*

Case Study - UKPRD835 - Metrics Aggregate View

From the Metrics Aggregate View, I identify the three metrics with high flag counts and high flag ratio of interest:

> Current Open Cursors Count
>
> Current Logons Count
>
> Session Count

These are all related to connection and workload issues.

Next, I focused in on the Session Count metric individually. The Metrics Time-Series view of all values of this metric, both flagged and unflagged, shown in Figure 8-15, allows us to easily understand the periodicity of the metric trend. From this we can see high session counts every day during UK and US work hours exactly matching the problem description.

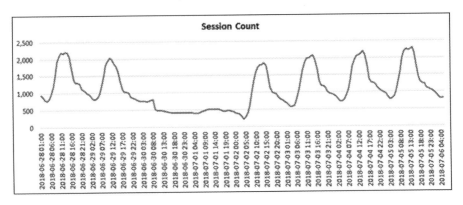

***Figure 8-15.*** *Case Study - UKPRD835 - Metrics Time-Series View – Session Count*

Further analysis revealed (among other things)

> Logon storms of upward of 20,000 connections per hour
>
> Lots of small SQL executions doing full table scans
>
> Excessive parsing (shows up in the Metrics Aggregate View, Total Parse Count Per Sec)

The conclusion of my analysis was that the performance problem was a result of the application behavior; it was creating a new database session for every window and running one or more small queries to populate data for the window [this behavior was confirmed by both the client and the vendor]. This is a common design problem with applications—it manifests as logon storms. The application had not failed earlier primarily because it was operating on a 40 CPU machine and had ample capacity to deal with the overabundance of connections required; eventually they ran into the practical limits of the machine. Since it is older hardware and not possible to add any more CPU's, the only fix possible is at the application level. This would involve adding a connection pool. This must be implemented by the vendor since it is a vendor product.

*What action did I take to resolve the issue?*

Advise the clients to work with the vendor to accomplish the necessary change in the application.

*Why is this case particularly interesting? What impact did the metrics analysis bring?*

The metrics give the clues to the problem, but it is still necessary for the analyst to tie this to the workings of the application in order to fully understand the problem. In this case, the metrics exactly matched the client's complaint, and this gave them leverage in working with the vendor. The DOPA process provided objective data that the problem was occurring as a result of the application and not the database and therefore required a fix at the application level.

# Case #5: Performance Investigation for Ill-Described Problem (a Narrative)

*What was the user's complaint? How did the problem manifest? Error messages?*

An application support client asked for an AWR report for a time range 06:00–09:00 on a particular day; it was supplied to them by a level 2 application DBA analyst. I knew that this particular application is important to the business and that the app team usually worked through the vendor for support, but my obsessive tuning disorder got the best of me and I began a performance investigation even though they didn't ask.

What type of analysis did I run with the DOPA code? Metrics flagged, interesting patterns?

I looked first at the AWR report since that is the data they had requested; it showed Average Active Sessions (AAS) in the hundreds (i.e., extremely high considering this database is hosted on a four-CPU machine). Up until that point, I had not seen an AAS that high so my curiosity was piqued and I decided to do a deeper dive.

The ADDM report showed CPU pegged and suggested adding CPUs.

The two tools I just mentioned are part of what I have called the "small model" arsenal of tools and were useful to a point, but I needed a more detailed picture of database to find out the problem and to determine if multiple areas were involved. For this, I turned to the DOPA process.

Using the Metrics Time-Series View (shown in Figure 8-16), I could see that CPU consumption was at 100% from 02:00 through 11:00 (see graph) [I learned later that operation DBAs restarted the database after 11:00 which cleared the problem]. Although the clients had indicated a problem window of 6:00–9:00, this view showed that the problem was of longer duration. Figure 8-16 shows a graph of the Metrics Time-Series View for host CPU consumption.

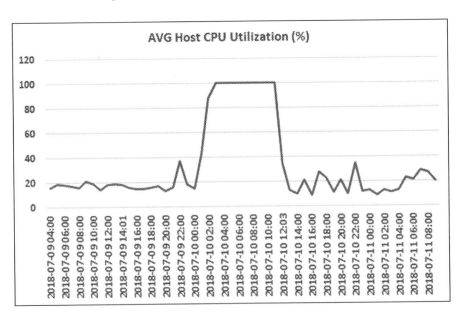

***Figure 8-16.*** *A graph of the Metrics Time-Series View for host CPU consumption*

Since the ADDM report also highlighted a particular SQL statement as high CPU consuming, I used dba_hist_sqlstat to better understand how this SQL statement had been operating historically. I discovered that there had been ~ 800 million executions of this query on the day of the high CPU condition. The SQL had execution times that were subsecond, but with the enormous number of executions, this added up to >24-hour clock time. I also found that this SQL usually had around 10 million executions on a normal, nonproblematic day with the same time per execution [and stable execution plan] taking only about 20 minutes or so of clock time in a day. Thus the problem was a result of an increased workload and not poor performance of the SQL itself.

Another iteration of the DOPA process using the Metrics Aggregate View revealed high values for the metric, dba_hist_sysmetric_summary: "Temp Space Used." This is an important finding as it is actionable for further analysis which will likely contribute toward a resolution.

What I did next was to analyze the SQL in the active session history during the problem interval, sorting the highest TEMP-consuming SQL at the top. I ran those SQL through the SQL Tuning Advisor to see what kind of actionable recommendations would be recommended.

Another metric identified as high by the Metrics Aggregate View was dba_hist_sysstat: "concurrency wait time" [this metric can also be found on a SQL by SQL basis in dba_hist_sqlstat (ccwait_time_total/delta), v$sql, and v$sqlarea; from the Oracle Doc's this is "The total wait time (in microseconds) for waits that belong to the Concurrency wait class"]. Since wait times are typically elevated during times of high CPU consumption, I am not particularly worried about actioning further investigation for this high metric.

*What action did I take to resolve the issue?*

My findings were shared with the application team. I explained that the workload had increased significantly as a result of the SQL statement running orders of magnitude more than usual, but that the execution time for each execution was no slower than usual. Thus, they needed to go back and figure out why the workload change had occurred.

*Why is this case particularly interesting?*

The DOPA process, as well as other small model tools, showed that the problem was related to high CPU consumption. The DOPA process enabled the deeper-dive analysis necessary to fully discover that the high CPU was a result of the workload increase and not the root cause of the problem. It also gave insight into metrics (Temp Space Used) that would have been missed using small model tools alone, and this insight provided an actionable finding with immediate performance improvement.

*What impact did the metrics analysis bring?*

Often time and effort are spent chasing symptoms and not the root cause. In this example, if the analysis had ended with the ADDM report, and the advice to add additional CPU had been implemented, the root cause would not have been discovered and resources wasted.

# Case #6: Example of Where Someone Might Think It Was a Top SQL, but It's Not

### OR False-Negative SQL Analysis

*What was user complaint? How did the problem manifest? Error messages?*

Application support client reported a problem that occurred in a narrow one-hour interval. The problem manifested as a SQL tuning problem. Using the traditional approach, the DBA performance analyst (DBA) assigned to this incident examined the top SQL that was present during that interval. In this case all the SQL executing in that hour had very fast execution times (AWR report, ADDM report, custom analysis of DBA_HIST_SQLSTAT). The DBA reported back to the client that the top SQL analysis for a one-hour interval did not show significant app SQL level issues (i.e., no resolution/solution provided). Further, there was no actionable advice from the SQL Tuning Advisor for the application SQL during the interval. I was asked to provide a second set of expert eyes.

*What type of analysis did I run with the DOPA code? Metrics flagged, interesting patterns?*

I began my analysis using the DOPA process and the Metrics Aggregate View. The DOPA process was used to reexamine the time interval. I discovered many additional flags on REDO-related metrics. The dynamically flagged metrics provided the information needed to direct further investigation. This further investigation led to the observation of blocked sessions and significant waits on REDO log file writing and switching.

*What did you do to resolve the issue?*

The solution in this case was to increase the REDO log file sizes.

*Why is this case particularly interesting?*

The DOPA process led right to the underlying problem which was not detected using the traditional SQL tuning approach.

*What impact did the metrics analysis bring?*

An essential observation was missed using the small model tools but was detected by the DOPA process. This led to a proper diagnosis of the problem and actionable solution.

# Case #7: Alert Log Example (Error Alert Failure Example) Narrative

*What was the user's complaint? How did the problem manifest? Error messages?*

Users reported ORA 600 error* while running a select statement. ORA 600 errors were also found in the alert log.

What type of analysis did I run with the DOPA code? Metrics flagged, interesting patterns?

I ran the DOPA process using a Metrics Aggregate View. The dynamic code flagged as outside of normal the following metrics from dba_hist_system_event:

Other: ADR block file write time_waited_micro

Other: ADR block file write total_waits

Other: ADR file lock total_timeouts

Other: process diagnostic dump time_waited_micro

Other: process diagnostic dump total_waits

These are all related to how Oracle internally handles the writing out of the ORA 600 error. They relate to ADR, the Automatic Diagnostic Repository, which is a hierarchical file-based repository for handling diagnostic information.

What action did I take to resolve the issue?

Since ORA 600 errors are handled by the database operations group, no tuning was performed, nor were there any other actionable findings.

Why is this case particularly interesting?

This case is interesting because the DOPA process was able to quickly identify the problem area. I wasn't able to determine the actual cause of the ORA 600 error, but I was able to determine that it was not a performance issue and was instead an issue with an internal process. This enabled me to refer it to the appropriate group for resolution without wasting valuable time on tuning, which would likely have proven ineffective in this situation.

What impact did the metrics analysis bring?

Because DOPA is able to analyze all of the available metrics, it is able to recognize problems not only with the areas familiar to most tuners but the inner workings of the machine as well. By quickly identifying the area, tuners do not have to waste valuable time trying to chase down problems in unfamiliar territory that can best be handled by others.

*The actual error message is:

ORA-00600: internal error code, arguments: [kggsmGetString:1], [0x7F54ADD62910], [13], [1], [11], [], [], [], [], [], [], []

# Case #8: DOPA Analysis of Oracle Memory Error—Narrative

*What was the user's complaint? How did the problem manifest? Error messages?*

Users reported an ORA-04031 error related to memory while running a select query (ORA-04031: unable to allocate bytes of shared memory). Usually this is something we would turn over to operations because we don't have the remit or authority to add memory to the database. I decided to run the DOPA process because I was curious to see how much information the DOPA process would provide for this type of problem.

What type of analysis did I run with the DOPA code? Metrics flagged, interesting patterns?

I used the DOPA process and the Metrics Aggregate View to analyze the metrics for the problem time interval to see which metrics in the infrastructure taxonomy and memory category were outside normal range. The following metrics were flagged:

dba_hist_osstat

- FREE_MEMORY_BYTES

- INACTIVE_MEMORY_BYTES

  dba_hist_sys_time_model

- Failed parse (out of shared memory) elapsed time

  dba_hist_sysstat

- Session PGA memory

- Session PGA memory max

- Session UGA memory

- Session UGA memory max

- Sorts (memory)

  dba_hist_system_event

- Concurrency: latch: In memory undo latch time_waited_micro

- Concurrency: latch: In memory undo latch total_waits

- Queueing: Streams AQ: enqueue blocked on low memory time_waited_micro

- Queueing: Streams AQ: enqueue blocked on low memory total_waits

These metrics indicate:

*What action did I take to resolve the issue?*

No action was taken since the memory errors are handled by our operations team.

*Why is this case particularly interesting?*

This example shows that the DOPA process is able to provide additional information related to and necessary to address this kind of Oracle error. In my organization, tuning professionals are not tasked with maintaining the actual performance of the machine, but for organizations where DBAs must provide all levels of service, this will be very beneficial.

*What impact did the metrics analysis bring?*

The DOPA process can clearly be used to get additional details on this kind of Oracle error. Furthermore, in this case the database experienced a very specific memory error, and the DOPA process was able to show that this event directly coincided with capacity exhaustion as shown by the unusually high value for the flagged memory metrics at both the operating system level (dba_hist_osstat) and Oracle internal resource level as well (parsing memory, PGA/UGA memory, latches and Streams).

# Summary

The case studies we've just looked at are a sampling of the types of problems for which the DOPA process can provide insightful analysis. I am persuaded that it can be used effectively for any kind of problem. Because it is metrics-based, it is an objective analysis, and because it uses all of the available metrics, it is exhaustive. When run in an iterative fashion, as I have shown, it can be used in a dynamic way to evaluate at the appropriate level to obtain information at both a macro and micro level. These are just some of the reasons the DOPA process is superior to small model approaches. That does not mean that small model analysis tools are obsolete. As you have seen in these examples, small model tools are very useful when used in conjunction with the DOPA process to focus in on problem areas. However, no other tool is as comprehensive, efficient, and objective as the DOPA process. I am confident that the dynamic method of Oracle performance analytics provided by DOPA will benefit every tuning expert who determines to learn how to use it.

The last two chapters cover monitoring (Chapter 9) and further enhancements (Chapter 10).

# CHAPTER 9

# Monitoring

Sadly, and all too often, we learn of database performance problems as a complaint from database users. Most DBAs and managers would like to stay ahead of performance problems by monitoring their databases and taking peremptory action to avoid the types of performance complaints to which most of us have been accustomed. Some level of automated monitoring is or should be an integral and important task for DBAs, especially in environments with hundreds if not thousands of databases, where the sheer volume makes it impossible to monitor manually.

There are currently many approaches to and implementations of database monitoring, and it is impossible in the context of this chapter to provide a full survey of the database monitoring landscape, so I will speak in a general sense on monitoring solutions. Monitoring usually goes hand in hand with alerting so that detected problems are pushed out to the personnel that need to action a solution. Most generic alerting mechanisms will support the ability to create named rules that specify an arithmetic expression of the form, <metric> <operator> <value>, where

1) <metric> is the metric that you want to monitor.

2) <operator> is the comparison operator to use.

3) <value> is the "threshold" value of that metric that triggers the alert (two values for warning or critical threshold levels are commonly used).

© Roger Cornejo 2018
R. Cornejo, *Dynamic Oracle Performance Analytics*,
https://doi.org/10.1007/978-1-4842-4137-0_9

When the expression that defines the rule evaluates to *true*, then the tool will send an alert. For example, one might want an alert when the dba_hist_sysmetric_summary metric "Average Synchronous Single-Block Read Latency" is greater than 20 milliseconds.

Years ago I implemented a consistency check system in Oracle for a large clinical trials system that used a key-value pair structure similar to that used by the DOPA process. In this system we supported complex expressions where the simple expressions could be combined into more complex expressions with logical operators AND/OR. For example, one might want a complex expression looking at two or more metrics at a time, such as:

Average Active Sessions > 4 AND Database Wait Time Ratio >= 80.

Since SQL is an interpreted language, it was fairly easy to get SQL to evaluate the expressions and return ***true*** (i.e., push an alert) or ***false*** (i.e., don't push an alert).

The problem with the typical metric by metric thresholding approach is that it is hard to know

1) What metrics are important

2) What values should be used for the thresholds and

3) What values are specific to a system or

4) What values are considered absolutes across all systems

Although some organizations may choose to build a monitoring system, as I did in the preceding scenario, it is also possible to use an off-the-shelf monitoring solution. Although monitoring products are available, most notably Oracle's OEM, they are not without cost or limitations.

*The Costs and Shortcomings of Current Monitoring Tools:* The total cost of ownership of a monitoring tool is always an important consideration; those costs involve not only any licensing and maintenance fees that may apply, but the cost of time/effort necessary for learning the tool, provisioning an environment for it, for implementing it, and for maintaining it. A tool with a large footprint might well be justified for large-scale enterprise systems, but for smaller database environments, the tool may involve more costs than the value it delivers. As I will show in the following section, *the DOPA process is a rather lightweight approach that can be used as a starting point to address many of the database monitoring requirements.*

When looking at the available monitoring tools, another factor that you need to consider besides cost is how well a particular tool will suit your need. The current monitoring tools have one important characteristic in common with current performance analysis tools, and that is they rely on a predetermined set of metrics and can therefore be referred to as small model monitoring tools. As with the performance tools, so here with the monitoring tools, they have "blind spots" built into them because they are only looking at a few hand-picked metrics. For example, the classical monitoring approach in older versions of Oracle (9i and older, but still being used by some DBAs in 12c) was to create shell scripts to identify problems and send e-mail notifications of them (e.g., tablespace size alert, UNDO or TEMP error alerts, operating system file space alerts, long running SQL alerts).

I view the small model approaches in both performance tools and in monitoring tools as "noise avoidance" approaches that keep you from being overwhelmed by the tens of thousands of metrics that are out there. The small model approaches focus on only preselected metrics because it is impossible to instrument many metrics manually (i.e., it is difficult to scale the small model approach). However, because they are using only a limited number of metrics, the small model approaches are only as good as the metrics they use; if the metrics used are representative of the range of problems one is likely to encounter, they can be helpful, but if not, you will miss valuable information. The "blind spots" are intentional and necessary without a way to process all the information, but I suspect the consequences are unintentional. The small model approach, by missing pertinent observations, can have the unintended consequence of allowing "mysterious," recurring problems in your database(s) to go undiagnosed and therefore not addressed in a timely way.

177

In my experience, the range of problems that one can encounter on an Oracle database is very diverse, so trusting a tool that uses the small model approach is risky. The problem is you can't monitor or fix what you can't see.

I designed the DOPA process as a tool for the Oracle performance metrics analytics use case; however, the many DBAs with whom I've interacted almost without exception draw the connection with the DOPA process and database monitoring in general. While I have not yet had the time to implement DOPA for this purpose, I am confident that the DOPA process would form the basis of an extremely effective monitoring tool and that it might be able to perform that function with less cost and fewer limitations than the more established tools currently available—at least for some organizations or in some situations.

As I said, you can't fix what you can't see, but using the DOPA process you can pull from all the available metrics, so I am confident that it has the potential to be a more useful monitoring tool once modifications for this functionality are built. The DOPA process approach may even be paired with machine learning to provide an even greater impact. I'll discuss that in the next chapter.

*Why the DOPA Process Is a Good Candidate for Monitoring:* As I've already stated, the intent of database monitoring is to identify, diagnose, and resolve problems before they create a negative impact to the business. Without database performance metrics, it is impossible to gain a clear picture of what is happening on the database in the background. The Oracle RDBMS is probably the most well-instrumented software on the planet, and the DOPA process takes advantage of this instrumentation. It not only exposes thousands of metrics but detects anomalies in the metric values. It is not a large leap to observe that the DOPA process could be leveraged to not only analyze and solve performance problems that have already happened but to inform your database monitoring and alerting decisions as well.

In this book, I have demonstrated the usefulness of the DOPA process for discovering performance problems. I have used the DOPA process in many performance use cases where the metrics are evaluated in the context of a known problem (i.e., correlated to a problem), and using the flagged metrics to inform my conclusions and tuning actions. With monitoring and alerting, since you are trying to preempt a problem, it may not be the case that the metrics are evaluated in the context of a known problem. This characteristic of no problem or unknown problem makes the monitoring use case somewhat more challenging as you have to be more confident in your conclusions and proposed actions. I will show in the following section how the DOPA process can be used to study metrics and develop this confidence.

# Development Requirements for DOPA to Be Used for Monitoring

In this section I will discuss in a general way the high-level requirements of a monitoring solution and how the DOPA process fits in.

Monitoring solutions all share some common features:

1)   Persisted historic metrics

2)   Monitoring and analysis of metrics

3)   Threshold alerting

In order to develop the DOPA process as a monitoring tool, each of these areas needs to be addressed/developed. I discuss in the following section some ideas I have about how that can be accomplished using DOPA. I reiterate, it is finite time that has prevented me from doing so thus far. I welcome any feedback from others who may have put some time and effort into doing this already.

1)  **Persisted historic metrics:**

The time-series AWR metrics instrumented in DOPA represent native measurements of the historic resource usage and are the source [i.e., "raw material"] that is fed into the analysis process. These metrics can be low-level information from the operating system such as memory swapping to more granular-level information from within Oracle such as latching, specific memory areas, and specific subcomponents of Oracle. DOPA surfaces this already persisted AWR information to help identify the root cause when evaluating performance, but for monitoring this ability can be used to mine the necessary metric data points during normal operation.

The DOPA process makes use of the persisted historic AWR metrics and provides a powerful analysis capability for drawing from any of the available AWR (and other) sources, not just those already predetermined by a monitoring tool. Using DOPA, the choice would be yours, simple SQL subqueries are all that is needed to include more/new metrics in the analysis, and with the built-in subsetting capability of the DOPA process, you can easily include more metrics to gain a more complete understanding of a particular area or fewer if you are only focusing on a particular area of concern.

DOPA is very adept at instrumenting and analyzing metric source data since this is what it is designed to do, but in order to use the metrics analysis for monitoring purposes, it is necessary to create a mechanism for persisting the results of a DOPA analysis as a metrics baseline. In the next subsection, I will speak to the analysis side.

2) **Monitoring and analysis of metrics:**

The DOPA process uses statistical methods to find performance problems by establishing normal ranges and then identifying metric values that fall outside of normal. This same functionality can be used to establish normal ranges for any metric. In order to use the DOPA process in the context of database monitoring, one would want to evaluate metric trends and normal/ abnormal ranges within the context of the normal operation of the applications within the database. This would involve a study of the metrics and "baselining" the normal ranges in the scenarios that make the most sense for your applications. For example, what may be normal on one machine will be different from another, and it may change over time—within a workday, within the workweek, and as workloads increase over time. It would also be quite useful to be able to run the normal range analysis for various periods (e.g., for the entire month, for the 9–5 time slot over the month, for the weekend, for daytime or nighttime workloads, etc.). The ability to sample data and dynamically calculate and persist normal ranges for designated periods and update the "baselines" on a continuing basis is something I believe could be accomplished with DOPA with some modifications.

# Persisting Baselines

As I mentioned in the preceding section, it would be necessary to be able to designate and store the metric normal ranges according to the period/scenario during which it was collected. You could persist normal range "baselines" periodically (weekly or monthly given sufficient retention period) over several periods and compare the normal ranges. You also want to distinguish between daytime and nighttime database workloads. This would be a tweak to DOPA if I wanted just 10pm–8am for a consecutive 30 days. The persisted baseline normal ranges could be used for a database or set of comparable DBs and then later used in the monitoring process for threshold setting.

Further, I would want to be able to identify the metrics as being obtained during "normal nonevent periods" as well as periods of performance degradation or other unusual situations (e.g., operating system upgrade X, application change Y, unusual event/problem Y).

---

**Note**   This persisted data could become the basis for "training sets" for further machine learning analysis/study.

---

# Further Thoughts on the Study of Normal Ranges

An important consideration in this discussion is: "How do you decide what is the normal operation of an application/database?" What follows is an approach I think would be a good start for establishing "normal" ranges for the database.

A starting point for database monitoring using DOPA would be to look at Average Active Sessions (AAS) with a focus on the time periods having the highest AAS peaks. To do this using the DOPA process, I would use the

Metrics Time-Series View, subsetting on "Average Active Sessions" and looking at all the values, not just the flagged values. For example, on one particular database, the highest workload period was between 04:00 hours and 22:00 hours on the 15th, as in Figure 9-1.

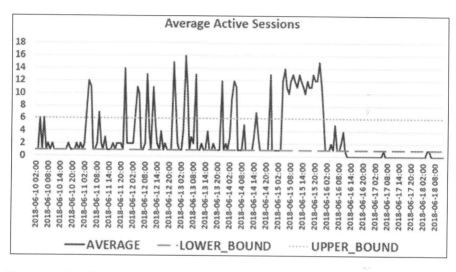

***Figure 9-1.*** *Average Active Sessions Time-Series example to find interval of highest workload*

Next, I'd take the highest workload period [04:00 hours—22:00 hours on the 15th] and generate the normal ranges using the Metrics Aggregate View.

The following example in Figure 9-2 is an extract of the normal ranges provided from the Metrics Aggregate View subset on source dba_hist_sysmetric_summary.

| METRIC NAME | LOWER BOUND | AVG All | UPPER BOUND |
|---|---|---|---|
| Average Synchronous Single-Block Read Latency | 1 | 2 | 3 |
| Cell Physical IO Interconnect Bytes | 189,517,276 | 1,022,035,811 | 1,854,554,346 |
| Consistent Read Changes Per Sec | 1 | 3 | 7 |
| Consistent Read Gets Per Sec | 15,844 | 62,504 | 120,399 |
| Consistent Read Gets Per Txn | 3,619 | 9,728 | 23,093 |
| CR Blocks Created Per Sec | 1 | 2 | 4 |
| CR Undo Records Applied Per Sec | 0 | 1 | 2 |
| DB Block Changes Per Sec | 24 | 394 | 1,012 |
| DB Block Changes Per Txn | 17 | 22 | 27 |
| DB Block Gets Per Sec | 32 | 399 | 1,053 |
| DB Block Gets Per Txn | 16 | 24 | 32 |
| I/O Megabytes per Second | 2 | 13 | 24 |
| I/O Requests per Second | 191 | 459 | 727 |
| Logical Reads Per Sec | 15,876 | 62,903 | 120,971 |
| Logical Reads Per Txn | 3,639 | 9,796 | 23,276 |
| Logical Reads Per User Call | 9 | 84 | 291 |
| Physical Read Bytes Per Sec | 2,237,483 | 10,059,697 | 17,881,911 |
| Physical Read IO Requests Per Sec | 221 | 343 | 465 |
| Physical Read Total Bytes Per Sec | 2,101,987 | 12,414,688 | 22,727,389 |
| Physical Read Total IO Requests Per Sec | 202 | 430 | 658 |
| Physical Reads Direct Lobs Per Sec | 1 | 16 | 37 |
| Physical Reads Direct Lobs Per Txn | 1 | 1 | 1 |
| Physical Reads Direct Per Sec | 167 | 452 | 1,178 |
| Physical Reads Direct Per Txn | 8 | 77 | 268 |
| Physical Reads Per Sec | 273 | 1,228 | 2,183 |
| Physical Reads Per Txn | 33 | 404 | 1,309 |
| Physical Write Bytes Per Sec | 278,919 | 737,174 | 1,540,131 |
| Physical Write IO Requests Per Sec | 2 | 12 | 22 |
| Physical Write Total Bytes Per Sec | 353,804 | 1,165,681 | 2,407,380 |
| Physical Write Total IO Requests Per Sec | 11 | 59 | 143 |
| Physical Writes Direct Lobs Per Sec | 1 | 2 | 3 |
| Physical Writes Direct Per Sec | 31 | 79 | 170 |
| Physical Writes Direct Per Txn | 3 | 15 | 42 |
| Physical Writes Per Sec | 34 | 90 | 188 |
| Physical Writes Per Txn | 4 | 16 | 45 |
| Temp Space Used | 216,648,284 | 231,429,678 | 246,211,072 |
| Total Index Scans Per Sec | 512 | 6,936 | 18,119 |
| Total Index Scans Per Txn | 160 | 540 | 920 |
| Total Table Scans Per Sec | 8 | 190 | 509 |
| Total Table Scans Per Txn | 8 | 15 | 22 |

***Figure 9-2.*** *An extract of the normal ranges using the Metrics Aggregate View subset on source dba_hist_sysmetric_summary*

So as you can see, the DOPA process can be used as is to help establish threshold values for any of the metrics. The process can be applied to single databases or across multiple databases depending on the need.

Again, I can use the DOPA process as is to study metrics across one or more databases to understand what ranges of values I could expect. For example, if I wanted to determine a typical i/o capacity in bytes/sec or i/o's/sec, I could build a model using the Metrics Aggregate View subset on metric_name like "Physical % Total % Per Sec" in metric source dba_hist_ sysmetric_summary in DOPA. This would provide a table as in Figure 9-3 that focuses in on the lower, average, and upper ranges. From this analysis I could establish a higher upper bound for normal by taking the max upper bound across multiple DBs.

| Instance | METRIC NAME | LOWER BOUND | AVG All | UPPER BOUND |
|---|---|---|---|---|
| A | Physical Read Total Bytes Per Sec | 2,285,580 | 9,052,605 | 15,819,630 |
| B | Physical Read Total Bytes Per Sec | 70,606 | 13,131,445 | 26,192,284 |
| C | Physical Read Total Bytes Per Sec | 8,734,960 | 97,077,334 | 249,279,332 |
| D | Physical Read Total Bytes Per Sec | 2,594,808 | 22,913,932 | 55,094,753 |
| E | Physical Read Total Bytes Per Sec | 9,987,474 | 51,159,372 | 130,050,637 |
| F | Physical Read Total Bytes Per Sec | 1,853,009 | 12,846,776 | 23,840,543 |
|  |  |  |  |  |
| A | Physical Read Total IO Requests Per Sec | 5 | 111 | 217 |
| B | Physical Read Total IO Requests Per Sec | 224 | 1,035 | 1,846 |
| C | Physical Read Total IO Requests Per Sec | 58 | 816 | 1,996 |
| D | Physical Read Total IO Requests Per Sec | 73 | 312 | 670 |
| E | Physical Read Total IO Requests Per Sec | 78 | 616 | 1,354 |
| F | Physical Read Total IO Requests Per Sec | 208 | 434 | 658 |
|  |  |  |  |  |
| A | Physical Write Total Bytes Per Sec | 713,161 | 1,286,192 | 1,859,223 |
| B | Physical Write Total Bytes Per Sec | 67,178 | 210,642 | 477,374 |
| C | Physical Write Total Bytes Per Sec | 94,560 | 24,342,636 | 77,096,254 |
| D | Physical Write Total Bytes Per Sec | 918,503 | 3,493,868 | 9,263,219 |
| E | Physical Write Total Bytes Per Sec | 6,854,128 | 41,561,853 | 76,269,578 |
| F | Physical Write Total Bytes Per Sec | 353,804 | 1,182,054 | 2,407,380 |
|  |  |  |  |  |
| A | Physical Write Total IO Requests Per Sec | 24 | 39 | 54 |
| B | Physical Write Total IO Requests Per Sec | 0 | 15 | 30 |
| C | Physical Write Total IO Requests Per Sec | 6 | 141 | 382 |
| D | Physical Write Total IO Requests Per Sec | 63 | 131 | 199 |
| E | Physical Write Total IO Requests Per Sec | 65 | 201 | 337 |
| F | Physical Write Total IO Requests Per Sec | 11 | 59 | 142 |

***Figure 9-3.*** *Example compilation of metrics across multiple DBs using the DOPA process*

In this subsection we looked at the analysis of metric normal ranges and noted that baseline normal ranges need to be persisted in a variety of scenarios and used to help satisfy the monitoring requirement of threshold setting, which is the next topic I will address.

3. **Threshold alerting—detecting a problem:**

The DOPA process does not currently have any mechanism for threshold alerting, but as outlined in the preceding section, the DOPA process can be used to facilitate this requirement of a monitoring solution by engaging in metric normal range analysis and using this analysis to adjust thresholds as necessary. Additionally, if you have a mechanism to set thresholds for a nighttime vs. a daytime workload, the DOPA process could be used to inform those decisions as well. For example, daytime applications might be more sensitive response time per transaction, whereas at night you could allow a slower response time, without sending an alert, since transactions at night are usually larger, longer-running transactions.

Typically monitoring solutions accomplish threshold alerting in two ways: by establishing absolute values for the metrics and by setting percentile values and driving the alerting off the percentiles. Each of these will be dealt with separately.

# Alerting via Absolute Values

Threshold alerting using absolute values requires that the absolute values for the monitored metrics be predetermined. The DOPA model-building process can facilitate this by supporting the study of metric normal ranges as described in the previous subsection. Even with a tool like OEM, the absolute values for metrics recommended by Oracle may not be fit for all environments, so the DOPA process could be used to check or set these values in your own environment. As described in the preceding section, you could use a simple rule-based mechanism to drive the alerting by evaluating an arithmetic expression/logical expression (i.e., <metric> <operator> <value>) and alerting when the expression evaluates to true. Such a rule-based approach would be an extension to the DOPA process.

# Alerting via Percentiles

Threshold alerting using percentiles is a more dynamic process that relies on statistical calculations of percentiles. Such a percentile-based approach would be an extension to the DOPA process. If I were to implement this requirement, I would want the percentile used at a particular alert level to be modifiable; for example, it could be that if metric values are above .9999th percentile, you have a critical alert, but above .98th percentile, it would just signal a warning. As with absolute value threshold setting, you must have one or more examples of typical workload or take your normal ranges from another comparator (like) database.

In both threshold setting situations, absolute value and percentile, you would want to be able to specify the number of occurrences required to set off an alert. I used the Host CPU Utilization % as an example in the preceding section.

Alerting is not all fun and games, there are some difficulties with alerting. For example, if you have too many alerts being sent, it could create a situation of "white noise" and allow something to slip by unnoticed. You can also have too few alerts, where, again, some important event slips by unnoticed. Therefore, I would expect that there will be some level of trial and error in setting absolute values or percentiles for alerting.

# Summary

As you can see, the DOPA process can be used to facilitate the monitoring process and with some extensions meets many or even most of the monitoring requirements. Further, the DOPA process's "big model" approach (or many metrics approach), along with the statistical analysis, makes the DOPA process a very interesting possibility for taking an entry into monitoring. The fact that the DOPA process has a small footprint and is lightweight and accessible also makes it even more interesting to be considered as a basis for a monitoring solution. I'm not suggesting that the DOPA process is the be-all-end-all with regard to monitoring solutions (there are many very capable tools out there), but in some environments, this might be all you need. For the ever-learning DBA, at the very least, the metric normal range analysis capability of DOPA (as described in this chapter) could be used even without monitoring to learn more about the metrics and their values that are most at play in the database environments in which they work.

Next, we move on to further enhancements in our last chapter together.

# CHAPTER 10

# Further Enhancements

## Introductory Statement

As I have stated repeatedly throughout this work, the DOPA process is something I have been developing over a period of time. I consider it an effective tool as is, but there are many enhancements and further applications which I would like to explore as time allows. In this chapter I discuss further enhancements/possible future work in a general way. I hope these brief comments will stimulate the reader to experiment with these ideas as well. If so, I would love to hear about the results of your exploration.

## Metrics Analysis

The DOPA process as currently coded uses a statistical process whereby outliers are removed prior to calculating normal ranges. The metrics are then compared to the normal range to determine which metric values should be flagged, and there is some ability to alter the sensitivity of the process. An alternate method for determining which values should be flagged, that is often used in monitoring, is to use percentiles. In this scenario, metric values would be viewed as a percentile of the high end of

© Roger Cornejo 2018
R. Cornejo, *Dynamic Oracle Performance Analytics*,
https://doi.org/10.1007/978-1-4842-4137-0_10

the range and flagged when in excess of the stated percentile threshold. Thresholds could be adjusted to create a greater (lower percentile) or lesser degree (higher percentile) of sensitivity, and because the threshold is calculated with each iteration, this is a dynamic threshold.

The PERCENTILE_CONT analytical function in Oracle could be leveraged to accomplish this mechanism for flagging. I believe this would be an enhancement to DOPA that could be accomplished easily. Although I do not have experience with other RDBMSs, I tend to think they would have a corresponding function for this task. The percentile threshold method may be particularly advantageous for metrics whose distribution is not normal. I am aware that metrics fitting this description are part of the analysis used by DOPA, but I haven't had the opportunity to investigate how many are normal vs. nonnormal in their distribution.

Ultimately, I believe that a meta-analysis/comparison of predictive models, one built using the normal distribution and one using the percentile threshold, could be accomplished via machine learning to ascertain which method yields the most accurate model. I'll discuss this more thoroughly later in this chapter when I discuss machine learning.

# Implementing Other Sources/Customized Metrics

So far in this book, I have talked almost exclusively about using the AWR metrics for the DOPA process, and I mentioned the possibility of customized metrics. Although my work focuses on the performance of the Oracle database, the DOPA process concept can be applied not only to other areas within the infrastructure but even totally different applications, essentially any set of instrumented metrics.

Following are some ideas about how you can leverage data from other sources to create customized metrics.

The basic idea is to union in other SQLs including SQL with calculated values. Any SQL can be a source of metrics including:

- Active session history

- Regressed SQL: dba_hist_sqlstat

- Advisor analysis: DBA_HIST_ADVISOR queries for recommended action

- Application of this approach to V$ tables and StatsPack

- Application of this approach to other metrics collection sources in the infrastructure

- Application of this approach to other database management systems such as Postgres or MongoDB

# Active Session History

To instrument the active session history and incorporate the results with other AWR metrics, I would preprocess the data so that the sample intervals match the sample intervals of the other metrics (i.e., the data prep stage). For example, to properly instrument v$active_session_history, one would need to know that there is one sample every one second [=> a sample approximates one second of DB time], and this should be aggregated to the snapshot interval (in most cases one hour). Likewise, to instrument DBA_HIST_ACTIVE_SESS_HISTORY, know that there is one sample every ten seconds [=> a sample approximates ten seconds of DB time]; again, this would be aggregated to the snapshot interval. In the case of instrumenting DBA_HIST_ACTIVE_SESS_HISTORY, which has "snap_id," it would be quite easy to obtain the DB time for a SQL statement in a snapshot interval: DB Time for a sql_id is (in the simple case):

```
select snap_id, 'sql_id: ' || sql_id || ' - DB Time' metric_name
, count(*)*10 average
, 'dba_hist_active_sess_history' stat_source
, null metric_id
from DBA_HIST_ACTIVE_SESS_HISTORY
where 1=1
  and sql_id is not null
group by snap_id, SQL_ID
```

Likewise, one could provide more details in the custom metric by adjusting the *group by*, for example, "group by snap_id, sql_id, event".

# Regressed SQL: dba_hist_sqlstat

Adding to the DOPA process, normalized metrics at the SQLSTAT level would be another possibility. Again, the process is much the same as for other metrics. I prototyped this instrumentation by unpivoting the multicolumn table format of dba_hist_sqlstat. Following the pattern described in the "Normalize the Data" section of Chapter 3, Data Preparation, the following SQL pseudocode (i.e., this is not the full implementation) is what the code section would look like when creating the unpivoted format of the active session history metrics of interest:

```
select a.snap_id, a.force_matching_signature metric_id
, parsing_schema_name || ': ' || sql_id ||': ' ||
'executions'        metric_name
, executions_delta        delta_value
, a.dbid, a.instance_number
from dba_hist_sqlstat  a
union
select a.snap_id, a.force_matching_signature metric_id
, parsing_schema_name || ': ' || sql_id ||': ' ||
'fetches'        metric_name
```

```
, fetches_delta              delta_value
, a.dbid, a.instance_number
from dba_hist_sqlstat   a
union
select a.snap_id, a.force_matching_signature metric_id
, parsing_schema_name || ': ' || sql_id ||': ' || 'px_servers_
execs' metric_name
, px_servers_execs_delta delta_value
, a.dbid, a.instance_number
from dba_hist_sqlstat a
union
...
```

Once you have created a normalized data set as in the preceding section, you would union that normalized data set in as per the pattern described in the "Union Data from All Sources" section of Chapter 3. Once the metric source is unioned in, you would then perform the typical DOPA process analysis on those dynamically created metrics.

The table in Figure 10-1 shows a selected output from running the prototype SQL code [the prototype code is not provided, as it is not yet fully incorporated into the DOPA process]:

| METRIC_NAME | LOWER BOUND | Average Value | UPPER BOUND |
|---|---|---|---|
| GPM933PROD: 4pma33wv11yhu: ccwait | 0 | 32 | 4 |
| GPM933PROD: 5chm2way44ktu: ccwait | 0 | 104 | 31 |
| GPM933PROD: 5v25a651p2xr9: iowait | 0 | 6647 | 1724 |
| GPM933PROD: 8vtffrcm2c9vb: ccwait | 0 | 44 | 8 |
| GPM933PROD: ah85nsr0pd5s2: ccwait | 0 | 14 | 2 |
| GPM933PROD: bfz3ph7au02bh: cpu_time | 0 | 7936794 | 2093316 |
| GPM933PROD: bfz3ph7au02bh: cpu_time per exec | 3333 | 7936794 | 1682128 |
| GPM933PROD: bfz3ph7au02bh: disk_reads | 0 | 36000 | 9448 |
| GPM933PROD: bfz3ph7au02bh: elapsed_time | 0 | 33066748 | 6947200 |
| GPM933PROD: bfz3ph7au02bh: elapsed_time per exec | 3732 | 33066748 | 6912569 |
| GPM933PROD: bfz3ph7au02bh: iowait | 0 | 26945470 | 6317906 |
| GPM933PROD: bfz3ph7au02bh: rows processed | 0 | 830 | 177 |
| GPM933PROD: bhmz4gf4w0ufp: disk_reads | 0 | 30 | 9 |

***Figure 10-1.*** *Example output from prototype instrumenting Regressed SQL using dba_hist_sqlstat*

So far, I've only done this in prototype and the results look interesting. I am interested to fully factor in this new capability into the DOPA process.

# Advisor Analysis: DBA_ADVISOR% Queries for Recommended Action

I have been exploring the content of the Advisor framework (in particular, the persisted data in the DBA_ADVISOR% tables) for some time now. I've become very familiar with the content and where to go for what kind of data. To me, the most promising starting point is the ADDM Advisor which has hourly runs that match the snapshot intervals. Essentially what I would do is unpivot the MCT structure into the IRP format and then union it in with the other DOPA instrumented sources. Since these results are more along the lines of actionable tuning recommendations, I would probably just include them at the top of the Metrics Aggregate View, so you could quickly see what tuning advice was made by ADDM. I have not yet prototyped this approach, but I have the basic queries to extract parameter change recommendations, SQL Tuning Advisor recommendations, and Segment Tuning Advisor recommendations.

## Application of This Approach to V$ Tables and StatsPack

For optimal real-time analysis, the AWR tables are not a best choice since you only get rolled up data in the DBA_HIST% views every hour (or every snapshot interval). For real-time analysis, I would find a way to instrument select v$ views and use those as the source of the metrics for the DOPA process analysis instead. StatsPack views could also be used as data sources for the DOPA process if one does not have access to AWR.

## Application of This Approach to Other Metrics Collection Sources in the Infrastructure

The fact that the DOPA process is currently instrumented for metrics coming from AWR should not be considered a limitation of the approach. Rather, DOPA's analytics-based approach would work for any metric instrumented across the infrastructure from other sources. Essentially, if you can get metrics into Oracle, you can instrument them into the DOPA process. Typically, DBAs don't have remit or authority or tools that cut across the infrastructure, but imagine if the operating system, network, storage, app server, and even application metrics were instrumented in such a way that you could talk SQL to them. It would then be a simple exercise to normalize them and union them into the DOPA process; this would provide a great deal of fodder for analysis. With better infrastructure visibility, solving performance issues related to the database would be much easier.

# Application of This Approach to Other Database Management Systems Such As Postgres or MongoDB

I've talked to many DBAs who work with MongoDB and Postgres; these databases also collect performance metrics which can be queried. Essentially, if the metric exists and measures something relevant, it can be used for problem-solving in the DOPA process.

# Graphs

I am currently using three views in the DOPA process: the Metrics Aggregate View, the Metrics Time-Series View, and the Category Count View. I frequently manually graph data from the Metrics Time-Series View and the Category Count View. I think it would be useful to be able to generate graphs easily to help with the analysis.

## Time-Series Graphs

Although I am currently producing a time-series graph that I use in my analysis, the process by which I generate this graph is clunky and time-consuming. It involves several steps: First I look at the results of running the Metrics Aggregate View and select a metric of interest, and then I use the metric name in a run of the Metrics Time-Series View (changing some of the parameters so that I can see all the data). Running the Metrics Time-Series View produces a table of data that I save off to Excel. I go into Excel and choose the columns I want to graph and tweak the size/fonts to obtain the finished graph. This can take several minutes.

This has been my method to date because Excel is accessible and fairly simple to use, and I haven't had the time to develop a more streamlined process. I know other tools for graphing exist and could probably be integrated with the DOPA process to produce quality graphs in much less time and be more easily modifiable. Google Graphs is one option that I would consider. Ultimately, I would like to be able to have a regular interface with the graphs so that a graph could be generated with just a couple clicks.

# Metric Frequency Distributions

A histogram representation of metric value frequency distributions is another enhancement that I'd like to add to the DOPA process. I have prototyped a Metrics Frequency Distribution View going against dba_hist_sysmetric_summary. With this prototype I generate a table of data that could be graphed to represent metric frequency distributions visually. In this view, metric values would be sorted into "buckets" representing a specified range of metric value. By adding a few key calculations to the DOPA code, I could use the inbuilt WIDTH_BUCKET Oracle analytical function and group by the metric name and the "buckets."

*Prototype Metrics Frequency Distribution View*

```
select metric_name, bucket
, count(bucket) num_values_in_bucket
, avg(average) average_value_in_bucket
from (
select metric_name
, metric_unit
, average
, width_bucket(average, (min(average) over ()), (max(average)
over()), nvl(:num_buckets, 100)) bucket
from dba_hist_sysmetric_summary
where 1=1
  and (dbid, instance_number) =
(select d.dbid, i.instance_number from v$database d, v$instance i)
  and    end_time   between sysdate - 30 and sysdate
```

```
and       metric_name        = :metric_name
and snap_id between nvl(:start_snap_id, snap_id) and
nvl(:end_snap_id, snap_id)
order by end_time
)
group by metric_name, bucket
order by metric_name, bucket
;
```

Note on bind variables:

I run the code through Toad which prompts me for the bind variable values; I suspect SQL Developer behaves the same way. SQL*Plus is different, so one should refer to the SQL*Plus documentation for how to populate them using that tool. As far as the values go, follow the description/advice in the following:

- *:num_buckets* is defaulted to 100 if you don't change it via: `nvl(:num_buckets, 100)`.

- *:metric_name* would be any metric name from dba_hist_sysmetric_summary, for example, "Response Time Per Txn," "Physical Read Total Bytes Per Sec," "Current Open Cursors Count," and so on.

- *:start_snap_id* and *:end_snap_id* would be the range of snapshots that you are interested in; by default, if you leave these bind variables null, it will look at all the data in dba_hist_sysmetric_summary.

A summary of the number of occurrences for each bucket could be represented using a histogram (see Figure 10-2). A histogram is very helpful for visualizing the normal occurrence of metrics; it helps you to understand what is going on with the database. I produced the histograms using Excel against output from running the query in the preceding section for the specific metric name.

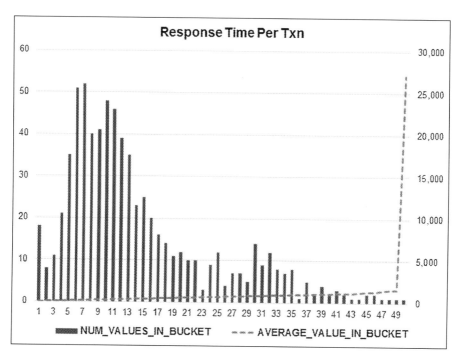

***Figure 10-2.*** *Example histogram: Response Time Per Txn*

Once again, I have been able to produce histograms, but the method by which I do so is clunky.

Adding a graphing capability to the DOPA process would make these tasks much more efficient.

Furthermore, since I've already normalized and unioned the metric data, I have access to all of the metrics in one location, so adding a Metrics Frequency Distribution View is not that difficult. If you tried to accomplish this task when the metrics were in separate tables, you would need several different pieces of code to accomplish the same task.

Many of the metrics I've generated histograms for have long tails on the high range of the metric and a big hump (or in this case two humps) in the lower range of the metric. By understanding the frequency distribution of the metric, we can project beyond the raw metric data at hand and make inferences about the metric in general even though we don't practically have access to all the data that comprises the true distribution.

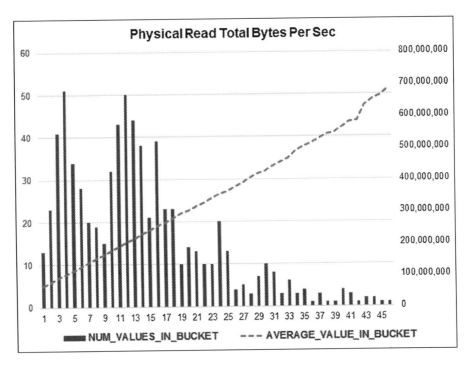

***Figure 10-3.*** *Example histogram: Physical Read Total Bytes Per Sec*

Another interesting perspective this gives you is the frequency distribution for the same metric across different databases. The following graphs (Figures 10-4 and 10-5) are for the Current Open Cursors Count on two different databases. As you can see, the distribution is specific to the database and date/time range when the values were collected.

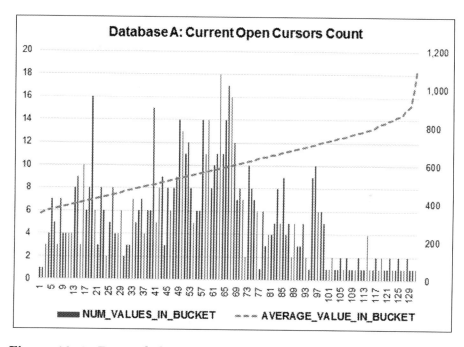

***Figure 10-4.*** *Example histogram—Database A: Current Open Cursors Count*

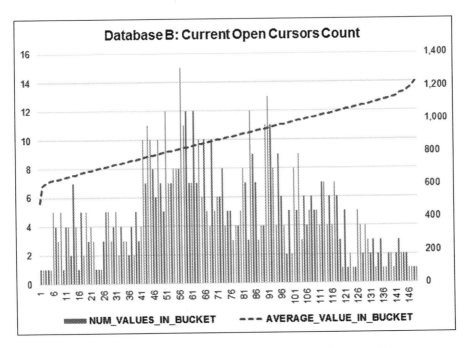

***Figure 10-5.*** *Example histogram—Database B: Current Open Cursors Count*

# Ranking

Given the enormous number of metrics available in AWR (as well as other sources), it is quite reasonable that individuals have gravitated toward small model approaches that are more easily comprehended. Using the DOPA process allows us to examine a much larger cross section of data, but even with DOPA it is sometimes necessary to prioritize. Here again, the propensity to pay more attention to the metrics with which we are comfortable is a real temptation. While experimenting/developing the DOPA process, I preferentially viewed my "favorite" metrics while simultaneously considering the other flagged metrics. This enabled me to see correlations with other metrics and gave me a better understanding of what was happening inside the database.

It would be a fairly simple task to manually assign a priority ranking to various metrics by including a column in the taxonomy by which the metrics could be sorted, so that when showing flagged metrics, the ones with the highest priority would be shown first.

---

**Note**   I have a thought that machine learning could be used to assign rankings rather than manually assigning them.

---

The idea of manually assigning a ranking/priority to various metrics might be seen as a move back toward the small model approach. I don't think that prioritizing is bad, I view this as emphasizing well-known/actionable metrics. Having said that, I believe there should be an objective method for bumping certain items up and ranking them as more important.

This leads me to consider another extension of DOPA that I think would be very useful—establishing correlations.

# Correlation Analysis

All database professionals already recognize the existence of certain correlations, for example, often when Average Active Sessions goes up, Host CPU Utilization goes up as well, or perhaps you have noticed when Host CPU Utilization is up, so is single-block read latency.

Since DOPA is already being used for statistical analysis, it is not a stretch to think that we might be able to extend its usefulness to methodically finding correlations between and among the many metrics, not generally, but in the specific performance scenario at hand. The correlation analysis could easily be accomplished using the correlation functions within Oracle.

The result of the CORR function in Oracle is a correlation coefficient ranging in value from –1 to 1. A correlation coefficient of 1 means that the two variables perfectly correlate (when one goes up, the other goes up, and when one goes down, the other goes down), so the closer to 1 a correlation coefficient is, the more correlated the two variables are. A correlation coefficient of 0 means no correlation and a correlation coefficient of -1 indicates the relationship is inversely correlated (when one goes up, the other goes down and vice versa).

---

**Note**   Oracle's aggregate function, CORR (var1, var2), takes two numeric variables as input and calculates the Pearson's correlation coefficient.

---

The fact that the DOPA process uses a normalized item result pair structure for all its metrics means that just one SQL statement is required to correlate all metrics to all metrics by joining the normalized metrics to itself based on the time the data was collected (snap_id). Of course, this generates a massive Cartesian product, so one might want to constrain the analysis to select metric names.

To test this idea, I did the following:

I suppose you could say I have a habit of developing performance tuning code in the "heat of battle." I was notified of a performance issue with a database where application functions hitting the database just froze. Initial investigation showed 100% CPU utilization for long duration accompanied by "cursor: pin S" wait event. The metrics for both "Host CPU Utilization (%)" and "Average Active Sessions" were extremely high during the same interval. Curious about how other metrics correlated to CPU, I created a prototype of a Metrics Correlation View (the "CORR SQL" in Figure 10-6 uses dba_hist_sysmetric_summary) to see what the correlation factor was between "Host CPU Usage Per Sec" and all the other metrics. Interestingly, I found some metrics that were better correlated than "Average Active Sessions."

---

**Note**    A session waits on "cursor: pin S" when it wants to update a shared mutex pin, and another session is currently in the process of updating a shared mutex pin for the same cursor object.

---

The following SQL code is what I used to prototype a "Metrics Correlation View." This SQL statement uses Oracle's CORR function against dba_hist_sysmetric_summary. This SQL statement will perform a pairwise correlation analysis for all metrics defined in the set "metric_set_1" against all the metrics defined in set "metric_set_2."

```
with snaps_for_interval as
(select distinct snap_id , begin_interval_time, end_interval_time
from dba_hist_snapshot
where trunc(begin_interval_time, 'HH')
between trunc(to_date(:intrvl_st_MM_DD_YYYY_HH24_MI, 'MM_DD_
YYYY_HH24_MI') , 'HH')
    and trunc(to_date(:intrvl_end_MM_DD_YYYY_HH24_MI, 'MM_DD_
    YYYY_HH24_MI') , 'HH'))
, metric_set_1 as
(select snap_id, metric_name, average, maxval
from dba_hist_sysmetric_summary natural join dba_hist_snapshot
where upper(metric_name) like upper(nvl(:metric_name1, metric_name))
  and snap_id in (select snap_id from snaps_for_interval))
, metric_set_2 as
(select snap_id, metric_name, average, maxval
from dba_hist_sysmetric_summary natural join dba_hist_snapshot
where upper(metric_name) like upper(nvl(:metric_name2, metric_name))
  and snap_id in (select snap_id from snaps_for_interval))
/* main select CORR function */
select s1.metric_name metric_name_1
, s2.metric_name metric_name_2
```

```
, round(CORR(s1.average, s2.average), 7) AS "Pearson's Correlation"
from metric_set_1 s1, metric_set_2 s2
where s1.snap_id = s2.snap_id
  and s1.METRIC_NAME <> s2.metric_name
group by s1.METRIC_NAME, s2.metric_name
having CORR(s1.average, s2.average) is not null
    and (CORR(s1.average, s2.average) >= .75
      or CORR(s1.average, s2.average) <= -.75)
order by 3 desc
;
```

Note on bind variables for the preceding SQL:

- *:intrvl_st_MM_DD_YYYY_HH24_MI*: provide an interval start date/time in the format: 'MM_DD_YYYY_HH24_MI'

- *:intrvl_end_MM_DD_YYYY_HH24_MI*: provide an interval end date/time using the format: 'MM_DD_YYYY_HH24_MI'

- *:metric_name1*: use a full metric name from dba_hist_sysmetric_summary or wildcard it with "%" (or any other wildcarded substring)

- *:metric_name2*: same description as with *:metric_name1*

Figure 10-6 shows tabular results of running the prototype of a "Metrics Correlation View" showing the pairwise comparisons of "Host CPU Usage Per Sec" compared to all the other metrics [:metric_1 set to "Host CPU Usage Per Sec," metric_2 wildcarded using "%" for a specific interval].

| METRIC_NAME_1 | METRIC_NAME_2 | Pearson's Correlation |
|---|---|---|
| Host CPU Usage Per Sec | Host CPU Utilization (%) | 0.9999996 |
| Host CPU Usage Per Sec | CPU Usage Per Sec | 0.9999934 |
| Host CPU Usage Per Sec | Open Cursors Per Sec | 0.9939273 |
| Host CPU Usage Per Sec | Executions Per Sec | 0.9939089 |
| Host CPU Usage Per Sec | Database Wait Time Ratio | 0.9936918 |
| Host CPU Usage Per Sec | Recursive Calls Per Sec | 0.9930246 |
| Host CPU Usage PerSec | Execute Without Parse Ratio | 0.9928608 |
| Host CPU Usage Per Sec | Consistent Read Gets Per Sec | 0.9897717 |
| Host CPU Usage Per Sec | Logical Reads Per Sec | 0.9896626 |
| Host CPU Usage Per Sec | Total Index Scans Per Sec | 0.971517 |
| Host CPU Usage Per Sec | LibraryCache Hit Ratio | 0.9591401 |
| Host CPU Usage Per Sec | Redo Generated Per Sec | 0.9563675 |
| Host CPU Usage Per Sec | Buffer Cache Hit Ratio | 0.9520388 |
| Host CPU Usage Per Sec | Disk Sort Per Sec | 0.9456909 |
| Host CPU Usage Per Sec | Leaf Node Splits Per Sec | 0.9406547 |
| Host CPU Usage Per Sec | Physical Write Total Bytes Per Sec | 0.9335514 |
| Host CPU Usage Per Sec | Physical Writes Direct Per Sec | 0.9326525 |
| Host CPU Usage Per Sec | Physical Writes Per Sec | 0.9316853 |
| Host CPU Usage Per Sec | Physical Write Bytes Per Sec | 0.9316826 |
| Host CPU Usage Per Sec | Total PGA Used by SQL Workareas | 0.9291835 |
| Host CPU Usage Per Sec | Physical Write IO Requests Per Sec | 0.9202646 |
| Host CPU Usage Per Sec | Physical Write Total IO Requests Per Sec | 0.8818121 |
| Host CPU Usage Per Sec | Cell Physical IOInterconnect Bytes | 0.8650617 |
| Host CPU Usage Per Sec | I/O Megabytes per Second | 0.8649289 |
| Host CPU Usage Per Sec | I/O Requests per Second | 0.8561682 |
| Host CPU Usage Per Sec | Current Open Cursors Count | 0.8443674 |
| Host CPU Usage Per Sec | Total PGA Allocated | 0.8200225 |
| Host CPU Usage Per Sec | Current OS Load | 0.8074681 |
| Host CPU Usage Per Sec | Average Active Sessions | 0.8073219 |
| Host CPU Usage Per Sec | Database Time Per Sec | 0.8073219 |
| Host CPU Usage Per Sec | Active Serial Sessions | 0.8066739 |
| Host CPU Usage Per Sec | Average Synchronous Single-Block Read Latency | 0.7633705 |
| Host CPU Usage Per Sec | Temp Space Used | 0.7548237 |
| Host CPU Usage Per Sec | SQL Service Response Time | - 0.8736485 |
| Host CPU Usage Per Sec | Memory Sorts Ratio | - 0.9126491 |
| Host CPU Usage Per Sec | LibraryCache Miss Ratio | - 0.9511274 |
| Host CPU Usage Per Sec | Rows Per Sort | - 0.9540155 |
| Host CPU Usage Per Sec | User Calls Ratio | - 0.9744004 |
| Host CPU Usage Per Sec | Database CPU Time Ratio | - 0.9944923 |

***Figure 10-6.*** *Tabular results of running the prototype of a "Metrics Correlation View"*

In reviewing the table (Figure 10-6), one can see that "Host CPU Usage Per Sec" is almost perfectly correlated with "Host CPU Utilization (%)" and "CPU Usage Per Sec." These correlations are not very interesting since they are pretty much measuring the same thing. The third highest correlation ("Host CPU Usage Per Sec" correlated to "Open Cursors Per Sec," with correlation coefficient ~ 0.99) is interesting though since the "cursor: pin S" wait event has to do with SQL processing (cursors are used to process SQL). Further, I discovered that the "Average Active Sessions" was not as well correlated to "Host CPU Usage Per Sec" as I thought it would be, with a correlation coefficient of ~ 0.81.

My current thinking for extending DOPA for correlation analysis is that the simple pairwise correlation analysis could be another view, say, the Metrics Correlation View, that produces a table of the pairwise correlation analysis. Such a view added to the set of DOPA model generating views should yield a higher-quality analysis of the performance problems and contribute to improvement in model accuracy. In addition, I could add a Metric Correlation Time-Series View, the output of which could be used to produce a graph of the pairwise correlated metrics on the same graph. The following graph shows an example of pairwise correlated metrics on the same graph for Host CPU Usage Per Sec compared to Open Cursors Per Sec, generated for the problem described in the preceding section.

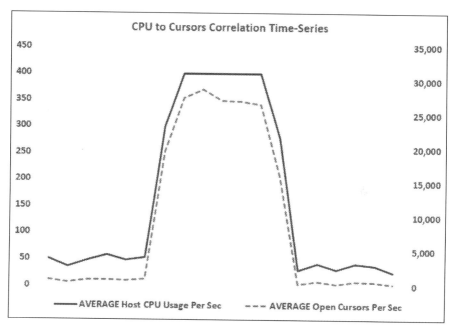

**Figure 10-7.** *Metrics Correlation Time-Series graph example*

In the preceding problem case study, the DOPA process was used to aid in the analysis of the problem (which turned out to be a flaw in the application which ran a particular SQL statement 800 million times in a day, when it would normally run around 10 million times). Further, the amount of SQL code needed to provide the prototypes of Metrics Correlation and the Metric Correlation Time-Series Views was not that much, and the impact of the additional analysis was significant in developing an understanding of the performance problem at hand. I am confident that adding correlation analysis to the DOPA process will be a fruitful endeavor.

Further efforts at finding correlations and assigning ranking might be accomplished via machine learning, which I will discuss next.

# Machine Learning

Machine learning is used in so many applications and across so many industries; I think it is safe to say that this capability is no longer state of the art, but rather state of the practice. Machine learning is a type of artificial intelligence that analyzes data to identify patterns and produce analytical models. Through an iterative process in which the models are exposed to new data, they are enhanced without human intervention, hence the term "machine learning." The increased capacity of machines to collect, store, and process vast amounts of data quickly has accelerated this field of study.

DOPA is powerful because of the statistical analysis it performs on the data. It relies on several machine learning techniques to produce a very accurate descriptive correlation analysis that can be used for problem-solving. It is not, however, in the purest sense, a machine learning tool since it does not "learn" and extend the model to scenarios it has not previously encountered.

I think it is possible and would likely be very profitable to build the capability of DOPA such that it could perform true machine learning. Furthermore, using machine learning with the DOPA process should be fairly straightforward and well within reach of the average software savvy DBA through tools such as Oracle Advanced Analytics, Oracle R Enterprise, MatLab, R, Python, and others. These tools have popular machine learning algorithms already coded up for you. With these tools, the DBA can focus on arranging the input data and interpreting the results rather than the internals of the machine learning algorithm; usually only a few lines of code are needed to implement. Personally, I like the idea of using Oracle R Enterprise (within Advanced Analytics license pack) because I agree with the strategy of bringing the algorithm to the data rather than bringing the data to the algorithm [plus it is set up so the developer can "talk SQL" to the ML algorithms]. In my mind, Oracle Advanced Analytics holds great promise as a scalable platform for building performance analytics models. I can see, however, that there are cases where running R, MatLab, or Python outside the database would be a fair approach. For example, I understand that R can also generate SQL that can be run in Oracle for some common processing.

In the previous section, I alluded to areas in which I believe ML would be profitable. I'll expand on some of those ideas here.

- ML applied to metric analysis

- ML applied to ranking

- ML applied to correlation analysis

- ML applied to building taxonomies

# ML Applied to Metric Analysis

Machine learning is a well-suited approach to analyzing Oracle performance metrics, not only because of the volume and variety of data (many variables) but because the Oracle RDBMS is an extremely complex software system with many moving parts that interact together. Moreover, since Oracle RDBMS is likely the most instrumented piece of software on the planet, I assert that the quality and predictiveness of the input data to start with is very high (many data mining/data analysis projects require a lot of data prep/cleanup work). The more advanced analytical methods of ML would likely allow a richer analysis and thereby yield higher-quality models.

High numbers of complex variables are difficult to study with traditional statistical methods but can be accomplished rather easily with machine learning. In machine learning, variables are the measures of interest; for DOPA, the measures of interest are the performance metrics. The promise of leveraging machine learning to Oracle performance analytics is to quickly analyze massive amounts of performance metrics, to find hidden patterns in the metrics, and to use that information for new insights into performance problems and even to be able to predict performance problems. The DOPA process already identifies the most important factors (metrics) through its feature selection/flagging outside of normal range; however, the use of ML algorithms would hopefully make the feature selection more accurate and provide a more rich association of metrics.

# ML Applied to Ranking

Since, broadly speaking, machine learning is inference based on data, it is quite reasonable to think that machine learning could be used to help rank which metrics are most important based on which ones were most highly correlated with problems or with predicted problems in the case of monitoring. This would be a good area to explore for ML. Sadly, this is an area of very early exploration for me, I don't have many details other than to recognize the potential for additional work in this area.

# ML Applied to Correlation Analysis

The DOPA process currently looks at metrics in isolation. The use of machine learning techniques should be able to provide insight into trends/predictive patterns with multiple metrics in combination. Using the machine learning approach of supervised learning with various problem types as the training sets, one should be able to obtain metric-based profiles of problem types.

The normalized metrics used by the DOPA process already provide a single consolidated operational data store which can be analyzed by applying advanced analytics, data mining/data science, and ML techniques. Again, the aim would be to discover key patterns and correlations from historical performance metrics and also provide actionable predictive analysis that could be used to reduce cycle time for a performance resolution, reduce application problems, and reduce downtime.

# ML Applied to Building Taxonomies

In a previous chapter, I hinted at building additional taxonomies such as a workload taxonomy (or building out the existing infrastructure and Oracle taxonomies). I haven't done this (or even completely refined the ones I have implemented) because building the taxonomy is a time-consuming process. It may be possible to use machine learning algorithms to associate a metric with a higher-level grouping to accomplish this taxonomy building process. The possibility of enhancing the accuracy and usefulness of taxonomies in the DOPA process via machine learning is another area that interests me— the goal with both of these being a better bundling of metrics.

> **Note**    A workload taxonomy could be useful in grouping the metrics into a set of workload categories such as storage/memory utilization, transaction rates, execution rates, logon rates, IOPS, and so on.

# ML Applied to Capacity Planning

Performance problems or infrastructure capacity issues are not easy to correct quickly (i.e., may require provisioning of additional infrastructure). For some performance/capacity issues and business models, it is necessary to know far in advance of an actual bottleneck what the capacity needs are and will be in the future in order to avoid problems that negatively impact the business.

The best way to avoid problems is to anticipate capacity needs and plan for them, but without the ability to predict capacity needs accurately, it is possible to either underprovision (thereby incurring the problem we were trying to avoid in the first place) or overprovision the hardware configuration. Overprovisioning may avoid the bottleneck we were trying to avoid, but it entails much higher operating costs.

With a good, metrics-based capacity planning capability, organizations can avoid both under- and overprovisioning and feel confident that the hardware purchase being made will be suitable for the intended use. I would venture to guess that in most organizations, such a capability would be a transformational change resulting in much lower costs.

Capacity planning is yet another area where ML appears to hold great promise for providing the insight necessary for making good decisions.

# ML Summary

Machine learning is now state of the practice and holds great promise for analysis and interpretation of big data. DOPA uses the data set of metrics contained in AWR to perform statistical analysis, but I believe that there are many more opportunities for using ML techniques within the DOPA process that would lead to even more accurate analysis and monitoring.

In the process of developing the DOPA process, I have been convinced of the "illusion of explanatory depth," which refers to the phenomena of thinking you fully understand something when you really don't. The more I learn about databases through using the DOPA process, the more I realize what I didn't understand before. I think bringing ML into the data analysis will yield great insights into database performance and show us all things we never knew before that will be very useful for the jobs we do every day.

# Chapter Summary

I first came up with the idea for the DOPA process around May of 2017. I started out prototyping using dba_hist_sysmetric_summary because the data was already "normalized." As I continued developing the DOPA process (adding data sources, converting cumulatives into deltas, removing outliers, subsetting on flag ratio, etc.), and using DOPA to solve real-world performance issues (often in the "heat of battle"), I became absolutely drawn to this process, and ideas for future enhancements would frequently spring to mind. I paused major development on the DOPA process so that I could focus on not only using and proving out what I had so far but spreading the word at industry conferences (Hotsos 2018, Collaborate 2018, ECO 2018) and writing this book. I am really jazzed up about implementing the Metrics Correlation View since the prototype with dba_hist_sysmetric_summary went so well. Further, the graphs I was able to easily generate using the prototype version of the Metric Correlation Time-Series View have helped me explain several tricky performance cases. Another area I have an intense interest in pursuing is the metric value frequency distributions and generating the graphs. The prototype for this has given me more insight into the metric data distribution than I initially thought it would. Moreover, I look forward to being able to dive deeper into the field of machine learning and leveraging this "state of the practice" capability in the DOPA process. There is much to explore, learn, and implement and many more fires to fight and problems to solve.

As I stated in the beginning of this chapter, I hope these brief comments will stimulate the reader to experiment with these ideas as well. If so, I would love to hear about the results of your exploration.

# Index

## A, B

Absolute values, 187
Active session history (ASH)
      reports, 193–194
  design, 10
  performance
     degradation, 10
  SQL statements, 9
  tools, 9
Automaticed database
     diagnostics and
     monitoring (ADDM)
  description, 13
  limitations, 14
  memory, 14
  performance, 14
  report, 13
  SQL statements, 14
Automaticed Workload
     Repository (AWR), 3
  data sets, 10
  data sources, 34
  load profile section, 12
  metrics, 12–13
  Redo size, 11
  reports, 10
Average active sessions
     (AAS), 165, 182, 206

## C

Case studies
  alert log example, 169–170
  configuration problem
    ADDM report excerpt, 153
    category count view, 148–149
    leaf node splits, 154
    log file, 152–153
    metrics aggregate
     view, 149–150
    resource manager
     metrics, 154–155
    surrogate metric, 151
  CPU problem
    CPU utilization
     graph, 159, 161–162
    metrics aggregate
     view, 157–158
    metrics-based analysis, 161
    metrics category
     count view, 156–157
    metrics time-series view, 159
    time ratio graph, 160
  server busy errors
    DOPA process, 165
    metrics aggregate view, 163
    metrics time-series view, 164
  SQL tuning problem, 168–169

Printed in the United States
By Bookmasters